MIXED PUZZLES

OVER **400** CHALLENGING PUZZLES

Bath • New York • Singapore • Hong Kong • Cologne • Delhi
Melbourne • Amsterdam • Johannesburg • Shenzhen

First published by Parragon in 2013

Parragon
Chartist House
15—17 Trim Street
Bath BA1 1HA, UK
www.parragon.com

ISBN 978-1-4723-1067-5

Printed in China

Fillomino

Fill every empty square with a number of any value. Each number must form part of a continuous region of squares of size specified by the number. Two different regions with the same number of squares cannot touch horizontally/vertically. Some regions may have no preprinted numbers at all, while others may have multiple preprinted numbers.

6	6	6	6	6	2
6	7	7	1	4	2
7	7	7	4	4	4
6	6	7	7	3	3
6	6	6	5	5	3
2	2	2	5	5	5

Find The Mines

		2					0
2					1	1	
1		1		2			
			1			3	
	1	1			1	4	
1				1		2	
	2	2		2		4	
			1				

Find all the mines in the grid. Numbers in certain squares indicate how many mines there are in the neighboring squares, including diagonally touching squares. Mines cannot be placed in squares with numbers.

3

ABCDoku

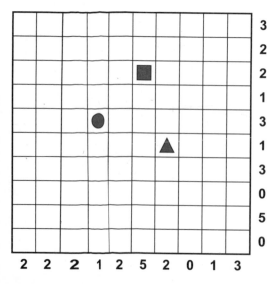

Each square contains a letter and a number. Place 1–5 and A–E once in each row and column to fill the grid. Each combination from A1 through to E5 also appears exactly once in the puzzle.

Battleships

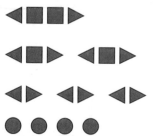

Locate the position of each of the ships listed below. Numbers around the edge tell you the number of ship segments in each row and column of the puzzle. Ships are surrounded on all sides by water, including diagonally.

4

Kakuro

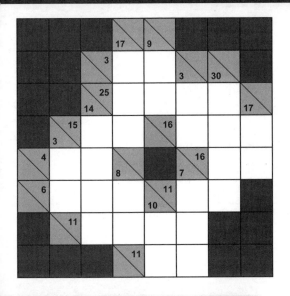

Fill the white squares so that the total in each across or down run of cells matches the total at the start of that run. You must use the numbers from 1–9 only and cannot repeat a number in a run.

Snakeword

Can you find the nine-letter snakeword hidden in this grid? The nine letters form a continuous line passing through each cell once without crossing itself.

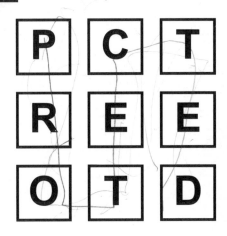

5

Word Square

Stated

Singing voice

Single article

Concave roof

Place four four-letter words to solve each clue such that the words are spelled out both across and down in each of the four rows and columns.

Diamond 24

The sum of the six triangles that compose each hexagon is 24. Can you place numbers from 1–9 in each empty triangle to complete the puzzle? You cannot repeat a number within a hexagon.

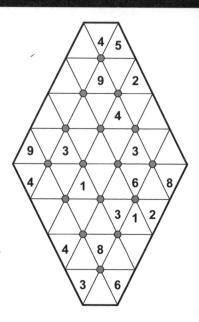

Dominoes

3	5	2	2	1	1	1	2
2	1	2	4	6	6	3	6
3	1	5	1	6	4	5	5
4	5	5	6	6	0	1	6
5	3	0	0	0	4	0	0
2	2	4	4	3	4	6	1
3	0	3	2	3	4	5	0

Place a full set of regular dominoes into this grid, where 0 represents a blank. Use the chart alongside to tick off the dominoes you've already placed. Each domino is used once only.

0	1	2	3	4	5	6	
							0
							1
							2
							3
							4
							5
							6

Futoshiki

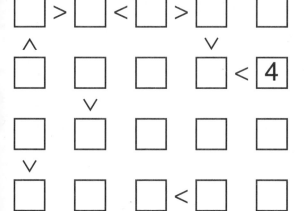

Place the numbers 1–5 exactly once in each row and column. The greater than and less than signs (">" and "<" respectively) indicate where one cell is greater/less than the adjacent cell.

Knight's Tour

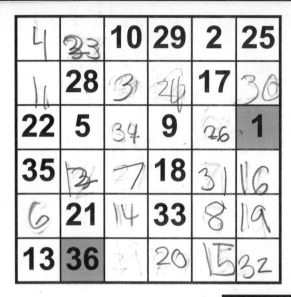

The grid represents the moves of a chess knight as it visits each square exactly once, starting at 1 and ending at 36. Work out the rest of the path of the knight and enter the relevant number in each empty cell of the grid. The knight moves either two squares horizontally followed by one square vertically, or two squares vertically followed by one square horizontally.

Pathfinder

Moving from letter to adjacent letter, can you find a path that visits every square and spells out the names of several words related to **getting married**? Start on the shaded square.

Divide the grid into a series of rectangles or squares, such that every square is in exactly one rectangle. Numbers indicate the size of each rectangle: for instance a "6" in a square means that square is part of a rectangle that contains six squares in total. There is only one number in each rectangle.

Killer 6x6

Place the numbers 1–6 exactly once per row, column, and 3 x 2 bold-lined box. Additionally the sum total of the squares in each dashed-line shape must match the total given in that shape, and you may not repeat a number within a dashed-line shape.

Number Tower

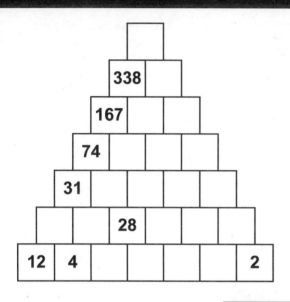

Fill the tower so that every square contains a number. The value of each square in the number tower is the sum of the two squares directly under it.

Word Ladder

Can you climb the rungs of this word ladder? Change only one letter at each step in order to move from the bottom to the top, and do not rearrange the order of the letters.

Symbol Values

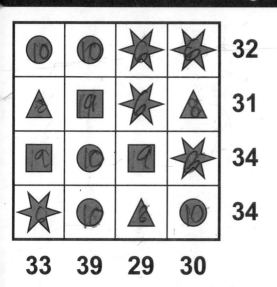

32
31
34
34

33   39   29   30

Each of the four shapes represents a positive whole number. The sum of the shapes in each row and column is displayed at the end of each row and column. Using this information can you work out the numerical value of each shape?

Word Egg

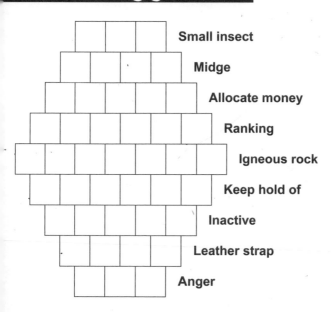

Small insect

Midge

Allocate money

Ranking

Igneous rock

Keep hold of

Inactive

Leather strap

Anger

Crack this word egg by answering the clue to the right of each row. Each answer is an anagram of the row above with either one extra or one less letter.

Word Definer

Can you choose the correct meaning of the following word from the options underneath?

DIMITY

1 A cotton fabric

2 A type of butterfly

3 An object made from diamonds

Wordwheel

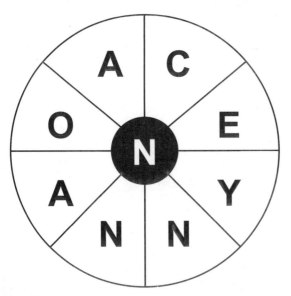

How many words of three or more letters can you find in this wordwheel? Form words by using the letter in the center of the wheel plus a selection from the outer wheel, where no letter may be used more than once in any word.

There is at least one nine-letter word to be found.

Can you rearrange each of these phrases to make a single word?

1 Tin peg ear

2 And bad one

3 Riper tent

Find The Sum

39	**27**	**25**
14 29	**38**	**22**
	32	
15 13		
37 24		

Three of the numbers in this box add up to 58. But can you work out what those three numbers are?

ABC Logic

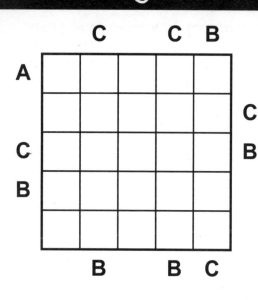

Place the letters A, B, and C exactly once in each row and column. Each row and column has two blank cells. The letters at the edge of a row/column indicate which of the letters is the first/last to appear in that row/column.

Binary Puzzle

Fill the grid with 0s and 1s such that 0 and 1 each occur four times in each row and column. The same digit cannot occur in more than two consecutive cells either horizontally or vertically. No whole row can repeat the same series of 0s and 1s as any other row, and no whole column can repeat the same series of 0s and 1s as any other column.

9+		6x			36x
2÷	6+	7+			
		120x	4÷		12+
2÷			8+		
2-			10+	5+	
14+					

Place the numbers from 1–6 once in each row and column, obeying the sums in the bold-lined regions. Numbers may repeat within the bold-lined regions. With subtraction always take the lower numbers away from the highest number in a region, and with division divide the highest number by the lower numbers.

Jigsaw 6x6

			3		
4			2	3	
	1	5			
2	4				
		1			

Place the numbers 1–6 once in each row, column, and bold-lined jigsaw region composed of six cells.

King's Journey

48	49		10	8	6	
46						
45				13	1	3
	41					
29		37				
	28		33		20	
26			23			17

Deduce the journey of a chess king as it visits each square of the grid exactly once, starting at 1 and ending at 49. The king may move one square at a time in any direction, including diagonally.

Dominoes

0	6	1	4	0	6	2	4
0	5	5	2	4	5	0	1
1	2	3	1	3	1	5	5
3	6	3	1	6	0	6	4
3	2	1	2	6	5	2	5
1	0	3	3	2	2	5	0
0	4	6	3	4	4	6	4

Place a full set of regular dominoes into this grid, where 0 represents a blank. Use the chart alongside to tick off the dominoes you've already placed. Each domino is used once only.

0	1	2	3	4	5	6	
							0
							1
							2
							3
							4
							5
							6

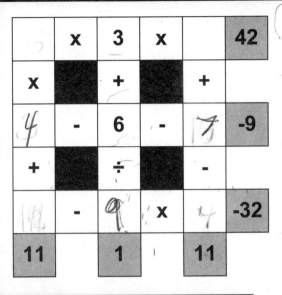

Enter the remaining numbers from 1–9 once in each of the empty squares to complete the sums correctly. Perform calculations from left to right and from top to bottom.

Symbol Values

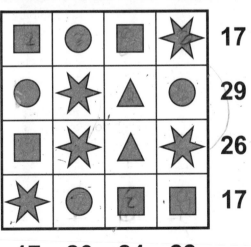

Each of the four shapes represents a positive whole number. The sum of the shapes in each row and column is displayed at the end of each row and column. Using this information can you work out the numerical value of each shape?

17

Scales

Two stars weigh the same as five triangles. One triangle weighs the same as two squares, while one square weighs the same as four circles.

Given this:

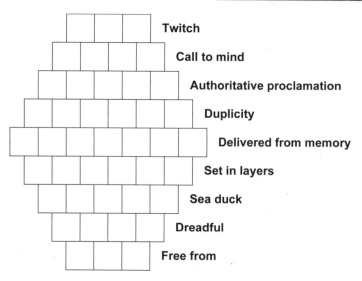

1 How many squares balance with one star?

2 How many circles balance with five triangles?

3 Ten squares and forty circles are placed on the left side of the scales. How many triangles must be placed on the right side for the scales to balance?

Word Egg

Crack this word egg by answering the clue to the right of each row. Each answer is an anagram of the row above with either one extra or one less letter.

Twitch

Call to mind

Authoritative proclamation

Duplicity

Delivered from memory

Set in layers

Sea duck

Dreadful

Free from

18

How many words of three or more letters can you find in this wordwheel? Form words by using the letter in the center of the wheel plus a selection from the outer wheel, where no letter may be used more than once in any word.

There is at least one nine-letter word to be found.

Word Pyramid

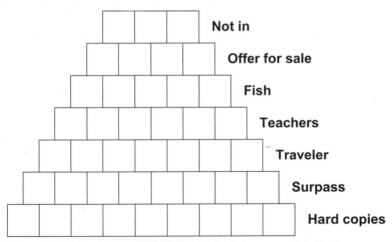

Not in

Offer for sale

Fish

Teachers

Traveler

Surpass

Hard copies

Fill each brick with a single letter to build a pyramid. Each row contains the same bricks as the row beneath but with one missing—however the order may vary. Each row must spell out a word that matches its clue.

Knight's Tour

		10		8	
		1	24		30
3	34				7
	27				16
21	14				
	36		20		32

The grid represents the moves of a chess knight as it visits each square exactly once, starting at 1 and ending at 36. Work out the rest of the path of the knight and enter the relevant number in each empty cell of the grid. The knight moves either two squares horizontally followed by one square vertically, or two squares vertically followed by one square horizontally.

Word Scramble

Can you rearrange each of these phrases to make a single word?

1 Yes dry tea

2 Arctic pal

3 No disc set

Each square contains a letter and a number. Place 1–5 and A–E once in each row and column to fill the grid. Each combination from A1 through to E5 also appears exactly once in the puzzle.

3	B1			
E	4	1	5	
	E		C	
			D	
	3			

Binary Puzzle

Fill the grid with 0s and 1s such that 0 and 1 each occur four times in each row and column. The same digit cannot occur in more than two consecutive cells either horizontally or vertically. No whole row can repeat the same series of 0s and 1s as any other row, and no whole column can repeat the same series of 0s and 1s as any other column.

		1					
1			0	1			
				0			
	0	0					0
				0			
0	0						
			1			0	1
				1		0	1

Kakuro

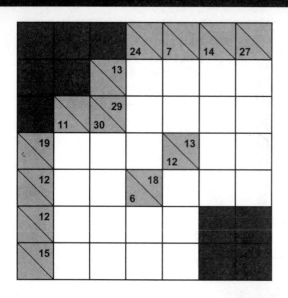

Fill the white squares so that the total in each across or down run of cells matches the total at the start of that run. You must use the numbers from 1–9 only and cannot repeat a number in a run.

Killer 6x6

Place the numbers 1–6 exactly once per row, column, and 3 x 2 bold-lined box. Additionally the sum total of the squares in each dashed-line shape must match the total given in that shape, and you may not repeat a number within a dashed-line shape.

9	14			10	12
	13	3			
			9	5	
12					10
	8		15		
	6				

Word Ladder

MISS

msat

Goat

GOAL

Can you climb the rungs of this word ladder? Change only one letter at each step in order to move from the bottom to the top, and do not rearrange the order of the letters.

Pathfinder

D	U	N	N	G	E	E	R	F
E	T	C	I	C	H	C	L	U
E	R	A	R	I	T	O	U	R
V	O	O	P	M	N	I	F	A
T	R	L	E	V	E	D	N	G
N	I	I	D	I	O	V	O	E
V	E	T	E	O	R	E	C	O
I	S	N	S	U	T	R	D	U
T	I	E	S	E	X	T	E	S

Moving from letter to adjacent letter, can you find a path that visits every square and spells out the names of several **character types**? Start on the shaded square.

Find The Sum

22			33
	35		10
14		30	
27	17		
12	24		18 36

Three of the numbers in this box add up to 96. But can you work out what those three numbers are?

Find The Mines

1			1				1
		2	1	1	2		
1					1		2
2					1	2	
			1		1		
3						1	
2			3		3		
		3		3			0

Find all the mines in the grid. Numbers in certain squares indicate how many mines there are in the neighboring squares, including diagonally touching squares. Mines cannot be placed in squares with numbers.

24

Hidden Words

Can you find the wines hidden in the sentences below?

1 Tiredness set in as the trio jammed all night.

2 Chaos at cheese festival as brie slingshot went wrong.

Battleships

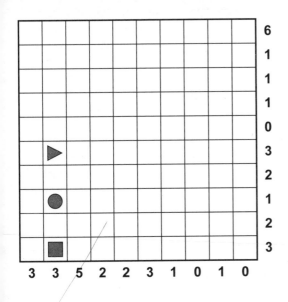

Locate the position of each of the ships listed below. Numbers around the edge tell you the number of ship segments in each row and column of the puzzle. Ships are surrounded on all sides by water, including diagonally.

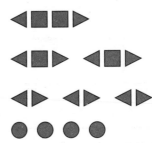

Number Square

8	x		x		64
+	■	+	■	-	
	÷		+	6	13
x	■	x	■	+	
	x		+		24
45		15		7	

Enter the remaining numbers from 1–9 once in each of the empty squares to complete the sums correctly. Perform calculations from left to right and from top to bottom.

Calcudoku

3÷		12+			3+
30x	9+	9+		12x	
					12x
3x	120x			9+	
	2-				11+
11+			3x		

Place the numbers from 1–6 once in each row and column, obeying the sums in the bold-lined regions. Numbers may repeat within the bold-lined regions. With subtraction always take the lower numbers away from the highest number in a region, and with division divide the highest number by the lower numbers.

0		1	0				
		1	1				
0					1		
		1			0	0	
0							
1		1	1				
						1	
					1		

Fill the grid with 0s and 1s such that 0 and 1 each occur four times in each row and column. The same digit cannot occur in more than two consecutive cells either horizontally or vertically. No whole row can repeat the same series of 0s and 1s as any other row, and no whole column can repeat the same series of 0s and 1s as any other column.

Symbol Values

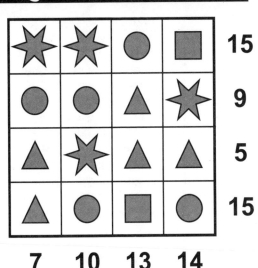

				15
				9
				5
				15
7	10	13	14	

Each of the four shapes represents a positive whole number. The sum of the shapes in each row and column is displayed at the end of each row and column. Using this information can you work out the numerical value of each shape?

Snakeword

Can you find the nine-letter snakeword hidden in this grid? The nine letters form a continuous line passing through each cell once without crossing itself.

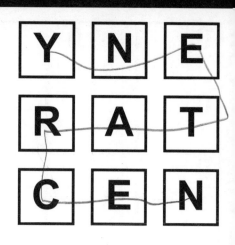

Sikaku

Divide the grid into a series of rectangles or squares, such that every square is in exactly one rectangle. Numbers indicate the size of each rectangle: for instance a "6" in a square means that square is part of a rectangle that contains six squares in total. There is only one number in each rectangle.

		3			4			5
		8				3		
18								
			9		2		10	
				3	3			
				3				
		2						
		2	2	3				5
							3	
	3		3			6		

28

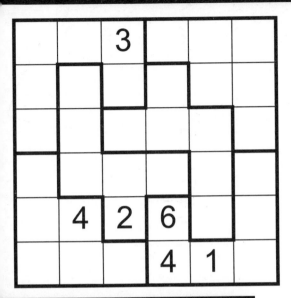

Place the numbers 1–6 once in each row, column, and bold-lined jigsaw region composed of six cells.

Wordwheel

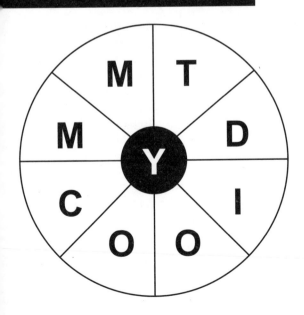

How many words of three or more letters can you find in this wordwheel? Form words by using the letter in the center of the wheel plus a selection from the outer wheel, where no letter may be used more than once in any word.

There is at least one nine-letter word to be found.

Fillomino

Fill every empty square with a number of any value. Each number must form part of a continuous region of squares of size specified by the number. Two different regions with the same number of squares cannot touch horizontally/vertically. Some regions may have no preprinted numbers at all, while others may have multiple preprinted numbers.

	6		5	3
		5		
3		1		1
	1		1		2
			7	
	6	6		7

Futoshiki

Place the numbers 1–5 exactly once in each row and column. The greater than and less than signs (">" and "<" respectively) indicate where one cell is greater/less than the adjacent cell.

30

Word Scramble

Can you rearrange each of these phrases to make a single word?

1 Eel on cart

2 Eager tuna

3 All energy

Knight's Tour

25	30	7	16	19	32
29	24				20
	1				5
	28	3			36
	11				13

The grid represents the moves of a chess knight as it visits each square exactly once, starting at 1 and ending at 36. Work out the rest of the path of the knight and enter the relevant number in each empty cell of the grid. The knight moves either two squares horizontally followed by one square vertically, or two squares vertically followed by one square horizontally.

Snakeword

Can you find the nine-letter snakeword hidden in this grid? The nine letters form a continuous line passing through each cell once without crossing itself.

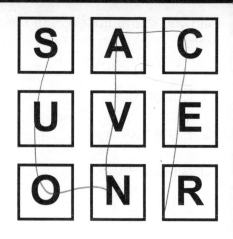

Diamond 24

The sum of the six triangles that compose each hexagon is 24. Can you place numbers from 1–9 in each empty triangle to complete the puzzle? You cannot repeat a number within a hexagon.

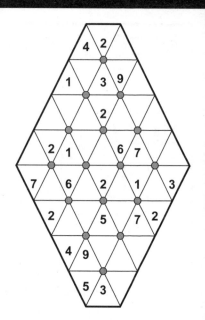

Four circles weigh the same as two stars. One star is half the weight of one square, while one square weighs the same as two triangles.

Given this:

1 Which two shapes weigh the same?

2 How many squares balance with four circles?

3 If one triangle and one square are placed on one side of the scales, how many stars are needed on the other side to balance the scales?

Binary Puzzle

Fill the grid with 0s and 1s such that 0 and 1 each occur four times in each row and column. The same digit cannot occur in more than two consecutive cells either horizontally or vertically. No whole row can repeat the same series of 0s and 1s as any other row, and no whole column can repeat the same series of 0s and 1s as any other column.

Number Square

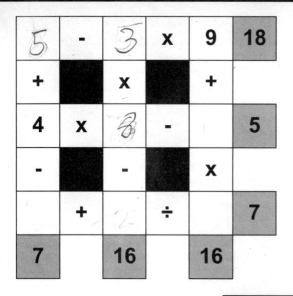

Enter the remaining numbers from 1–9 once in each of the empty squares to complete the sums correctly. Perform calculations from left to right and from top to bottom.

Number Tower

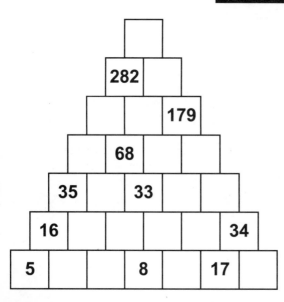

Fill the tower so that every square contains a number. The value of each square in the number tower is the sum of the two squares directly under it.

34

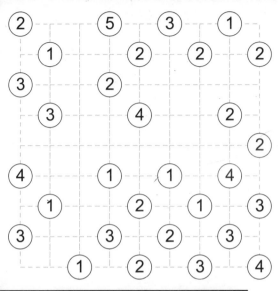

Connect all the circles (which represent islands) into a single interconnected group. The number in a circle represents the number of bridges that connect that island to other islands. Bridges can only be created horizontally or vertically, with no more than two bridges between any pair of islands. Bridges cannot cross any other bridges.

Killer 6x6

9			13	11	5
10					
7	9	6		4	
			11		
7		15			12
	7				

Place the numbers 1–6 exactly once per row, column, and 3 x 2 bold-lined box. Additionally the sum total of the squares in each dashed-line shape must match the total given in that shape, and you may not repeat a number within a dashed-line shape.

ABCDoku

3		5		
	A		E	
	B		C	D
			D5	
			1	C4

Each square contains a letter and a number. Place 1–5 and A–E once in each row and column to fill the grid. Each combination from A1 through to E5 also appears exactly once in the puzzle.

King's Journey

33		30	1			4
	35				6	
	37			11		7
		39		20		
	49		26		19	
43		47				
	45	24				15

Deduce the journey of a chess king as it visits each square of the grid exactly once, starting at 1 and ending at 49. The king may move one square at a time in any direction, including diagonally.

36

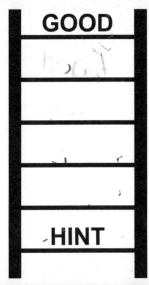

GOOD

HINT

Can you climb the rungs of this word ladder? Change only one letter at each step in order to move from the bottom to the top, and do not rearrange the order of the letters.

Snakeword

Can you find the nine-letter snakeword hidden in this grid? The nine letters form a continuous line passing through each cell once without crossing itself.

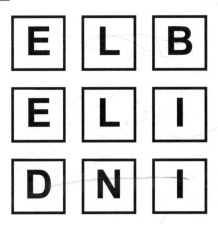

Jigsaw 6x6

Place the numbers 1–6 once in each row, column, and bold-lined jigsaw region composed of six cells.

5	2	1	3		
6	4				
2	6				
3	1	5		6	
4	5		1		3
1	3		2		

Find The Mines

Find all the mines in the grid. Numbers in certain squares indicate how many mines there are in the neighboring squares, including diagonally touching squares. Mines cannot be placed in squares with numbers.

1			2		1		
				1		2	
1		2	2	1	1		
		2				2	
2					2		3
		4		1			
2			2		3	2	
						1	

38

Divide the grid into a series of rectangles, such that every square is in exactly one rectangle. Numbers indicate the size of each rectangle: for instance a "6" in a square means that square is part of a rectangle that contains six squares in total. There is only one number in each rectangle.

	2		2				4	2
	2		6					
						8		10
				6	2			
2			6					
							4	
	10				2	2		
2		5					3	2
			18					

Battleships

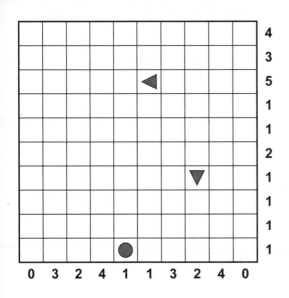

4
3
5
1
1
2
1
1
1
1

0 3 2 4 1 1 3 2 4 0

Locate the position of each of the ships listed below. Numbers around the edge tell you the number of ship segments in each row and column of the puzzle. Ships are surrounded on all sides by water, including diagonally.

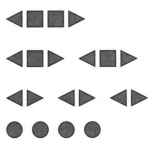

39

Kakuro

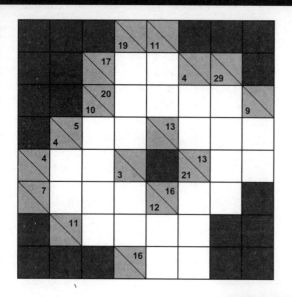

Fill the white squares so that the total in each across or down run of cells matches the total at the start of that run. You must use the numbers from 1–9 only and cannot repeat a number in a run.

Killer 6x6

8		12			9
10		4		8	
7	9		15		
		9			12
5					
	9		9		

Place the numbers 1–6 exactly once per row, column, and 3 x 2 bold-lined box. Additionally the sum total of the squares in each dashed-line shape must match the total given in that shape, and you may not repeat a number within a dashed-line shape.

Can you find the tennis-related words hidden in the sentences below?

1 Caviar club devotee had exclusive beluga membership turned down.

2 Trouble at the salon as hairdresser vehemently denied ruining the hair of a customer.

Pathfinder

O	C	S	A	R	H	G	I	E
M	R	E	T	E	T	E	P	W
P	U	T	N	A	C	N	A	R
I	C	E	A	M	H	I	P	E
L	N	R	L	X	A	C	I	P
P	E	P	P	A	B	R	E	O
A	P	O	T	F	I	T	O	C
R	E	P	T	E	N	O	H	P
C	L	I	P	S	L	A	M	P

Moving from letter to adjacent letter, can you find a path that visits every square and spells out the names of several **office items**? Start on the shaded square.

41

Number Tower

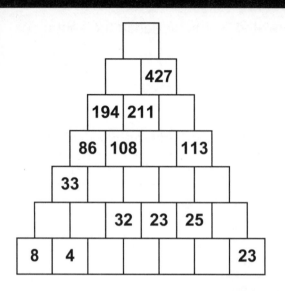

Fill the tower so that every square contains a number. The value of each square in the number tower is the sum of the two squares directly under it.

Word Square

Outside shelter

Chieftain

Pleasant

Arduous journey

Place four four-letter words to solve each clue such that the words are spelled out both across and down in each of the four rows and columns.

Bridges

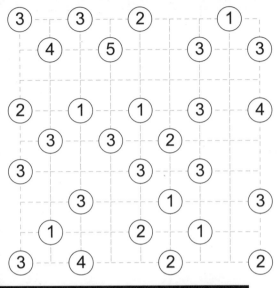

Connect all the circles (which represent islands) into a single interconnected group. The number in a circle represents the number of bridges that connect that island to other islands. Bridges can only be created horizontally or vertically, with no more than two bridges between any pair of islands. Bridges cannot cross any other bridges.

Calcudoku

5+		13+	6+	72x	
2-				5+	
	5+		16+		7+
108x					
1÷		12+		5+	
				30x	

Place the numbers from 1–6 once in each row and column, obeying the sums in the bold-lined regions. Numbers may repeat within the bold-lined regions. With subtraction always take the lower numbers away from the highest number in a region, and with division divide the highest number by the lower numbers.

Word Scramble

Can you rearrange each of these phrases to make a single word?

1 Site memos

2 Mum pro tip

3 Icy antler

Futoshiki

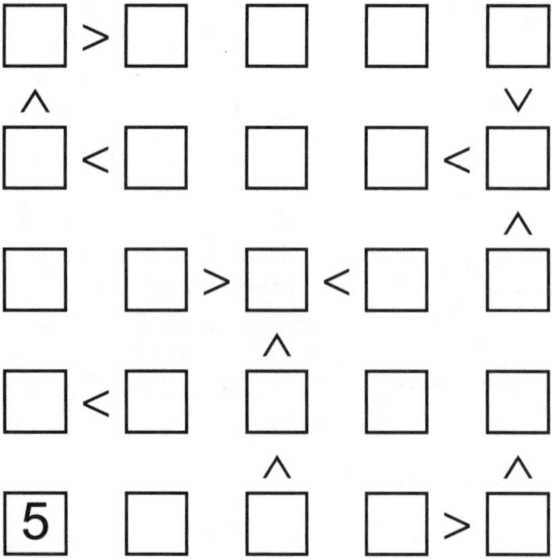

Place the numbers 1–5 exactly once in each row and column. The greater than and less than signs (">" and "<" respectively) indicate where one cell is greater/less than the adjacent cell.

Fill the grid with 0s and 1s such that 0 and 1 each occur four times in each row and column. The same digit cannot occur in more than two consecutive cells either horizontally or vertically. No whole row can repeat the same series of 0s and 1s as any other row, and no whole column can repeat the same series of 0s and 1s as any other column.

				0		1	1
1		0					1
	1		1			0	
				0			
0							
		1					
	1			1			
1					1		

ABCDoku

Each square contains a letter and a number. Place 1–5 and A–E once in each row and column to fill the grid. Each combination from A1 through to E5 also appears exactly once in the puzzle.

			A	D4
	A			
E				
			E1	
4		1	C2	3

Kakuro

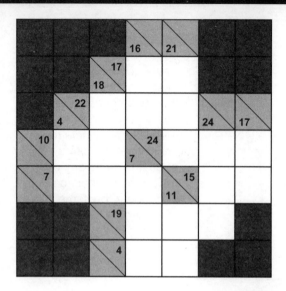

Fill the white squares so that the total in each across or down run of cells matches the total at the start of that run. You must use the numbers from 1–9 only and cannot repeat a number in a run.

Diamond 25

The sum of the six triangles that compose each hexagon is 25. Can you place numbers from 1–9 in each empty triangle to complete the puzzle? You cannot repeat a number within a hexagon.

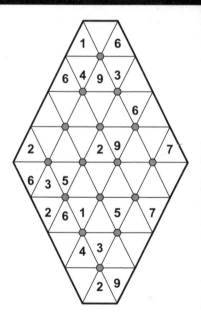

Fillomino

Fill every empty square with a number of any value. Each number must form part of a continuous region of squares of size specified by the number. Two different regions with the same number of squares cannot touch horizontally/vertically. Some regions may have no preprinted numbers at all, while others may have multiple preprinted numbers.

			1	6		
3						
6	2	7			1	
		6			7	3	3
						3
			6	6		

Find The Mines

							2
	2		4	3			
	3			2			2
			2		2	1	
	2	2				2	
			3				
1			2		2	1	
1	1						

Find all the mines in the grid. Numbers in certain squares indicate how many mines there are in the neighboring squares, including diagonally touching squares. Mines cannot be placed in squares with numbers.

ABCDoku

	E	D5		
	1			
C	5			
	C	2		
	B	3		2

Each square contains a letter and a number. Place 1–5 and A–E once in each row and column to fill the grid. Each combination from A1 through to E5 also appears exactly once in the puzzle.

Battleships

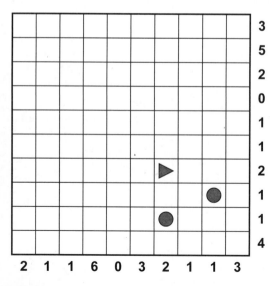

3
5
2
0
1
1
2
1
1
4

2 1 1 6 0 3 2 1 1 3

Locate the position of each of the ships listed below. Numbers around the edge tell you the number of ship segments in each row and column of the puzzle. Ships are surrounded on all sides by water, including diagonally.

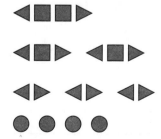

48

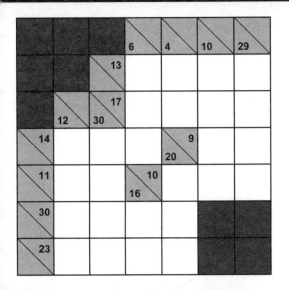

Fill the white squares so that the total in each across or down run of cells matches the total at the start of that run. You must use the numbers from 1–9 only and cannot repeat a number in a run.

Snakeword

Can you find the nine-letter snakeword hidden in this grid? The nine letters form a continuous line passing through each cell once without crossing itself.

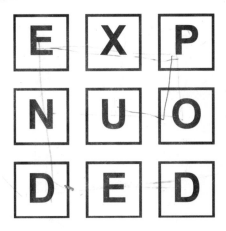

Word Square

Adjoin

Lead singer of U2

Reverse

Snatched

Place four four-letter words to solve each clue such that the words are spelled out both across and down in each of the four rows and columns.

Diamond 24

The sum of the six triangles that compose each hexagon is 24. Can you place numbers from 1–9 in each empty triangle to complete the puzzle? You cannot repeat a number within a hexagon.

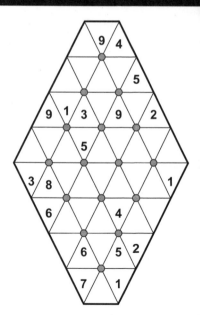

Dominoes

1	6	0	5	3	1	4	1
5	6	0	5	6	2	4	1
5	0	0	4	5	5	3	2
6	6	5	5	0	6	4	3
2	6	4	2	2	1	3	3
1	0	3	1	2	2	4	4
3	3	0	4	2	0	6	1

Place a full set of regular dominoes into this grid, where 0 represents a blank. Use the chart alongside to tick off the dominoes you've already placed. Each domino is used once only.

0	1	2	3	4	5	6	
							0
							1
							2
							3
							4
							5
							6

Futoshiki

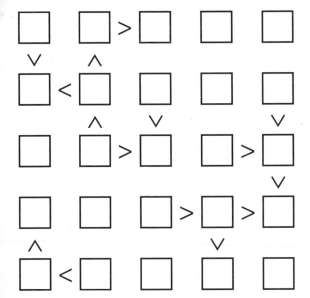

Place the numbers 1–5 exactly once in each row and column. The greater than and less than signs (">" and "<" respectively) indicate where one cell is greater/less than the adjacent cell.

51

Wordwheel

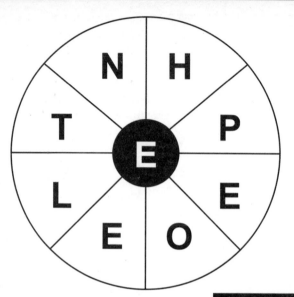

How many words of three or more letters can you find in this wordwheel? Form words by using the letter in the center of the wheel plus a selection from the outer wheel, where no letter may be used more than once in any word.

There is at least one nine-letter word to be found.

Pathfinder

R	A	I	N	E	R	J	O	G
T	S	S	O	R	C	N	I	G
W	A	R	M	U	P	G	S	W
S	G	N	A	S	I	U	M	E
E	Y	M	T	S	N	O	I	A
I	R	P	E	S	M	O	T	T
L	O	P	E	T	H	T	A	I
A	I	B	R	A	G	I	V	N
C	C	O	R	E	I	E	W	G

Moving from letter to adjacent letter, can you find a path that visits every square and spells out the names of several words relating to **exercise**? Start on the shaded square.

Divide the grid into a series of rectangles or squares, such that every square is in exactly one rectangle. Numbers indicate the size of each rectangle: for instance a "6" in a square means that square is part of a rectangle that contains six squares in total. There is only one number in each rectangle.

The Sikaku grid contains the following clues:
- Row 1: 8
- Row 2: 6, 10, 2
- Row 3: 4
- Row 4: 3
- Row 5: 18
- Row 6: 6
- Row 7: 3, 3
- Row 8: 9, 2, 4
- Row 9: 3, 9
- Row 10: 2, 8

Killer 6x6

Place the numbers 1–6 exactly once per row, column, and 3 x 2 bold-lined box. Additionally the sum total of the squares in each dashed-line shape must match the total given in that shape, and you may not repeat a number within a dashed-line shape.

The Killer 6x6 grid contains the following clues:
- 11, 9, 8
- 10, 9
- 8, 8, 7
- 11, 7
- 12, 5, 11
- 6, 4

Number Tower

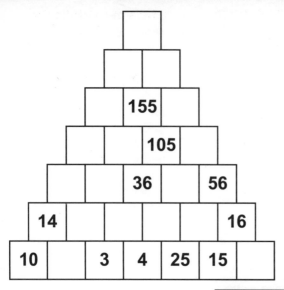

Fill the tower so that every square contains a number. The value of each square in the number tower is the sum of the two squares directly under it.

Word Ladder

DOGS

BARK

Can you climb the rungs of this word ladder? Change only one letter at each step in order to move from the bottom to the top, and do not rearrange the order of the letters.

Symbol Values

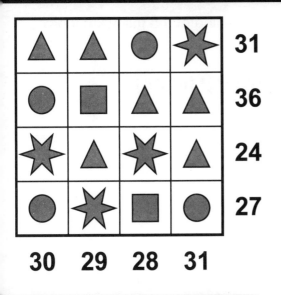

Each of the four shapes represents a positive whole number. The sum of the shapes in each row and column is displayed at the end of each row and column. Using this information can you work out the numerical value of each shape?

Word Egg

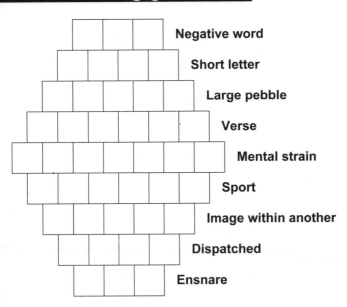

Negative word

Short letter

Large pebble

Verse

Mental strain

Sport

Image within another

Dispatched

Ensnare

Crack this word egg by answering the clue to the right of each row. Each answer is an anagram of the row above with either one extra or one less letter.

Word Definer

Can you choose the correct meaning of the following word from the options underneath?

ENERGUMEN

1 Tiredness

2 A fanatic

3 A mystery

Wordwheel

How many words of three or more letters can you find in this wordwheel? Form words by using the letter in the center of the wheel plus a selection from the outer wheel, where no letter may be used more than once in any word.

There is at least one nine-letter word to be found.

Can you rearrange each of these phrases to make a single word?

1 Not mad bin

2 Red snipes

3 Render aim

Find The Sum

32		34	
14	30	38	39
43			
24	23	33	
13	18		

Three of the numbers in this box add up to 108. But can you work out what those three numbers are?

ABC Logic

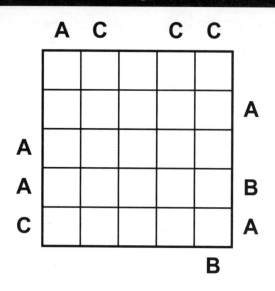

Place the letters A, B, and C exactly once in each row and column. Each row and column has two blank cells. The letters at the edge of a row/column indicate which of the letters is the first/last to appear in that row/column.

Binary Puzzle

Fill the grid with 0s and 1s such that 0 and 1 each occur four times in each row and column. The same digit cannot occur in more than two consecutive cells either horizontally or vertically. No whole row can repeat the same series of 0s and 1s as any other row, and no whole column can repeat the same series of 0s and 1s as any other column.

1-		12x			8+
4-		3÷	4÷	9+	
11+					12+
1÷		3-			
	14+			40x	
	8+				

Place the numbers from 1–6 once in each row and column, obeying the sums in the bold-lined regions. Numbers may repeat within the bold-lined regions. With subtraction always take the lower numbers away from the highest number in a region, and with division divide the highest number by the lower numbers.

Jigsaw 6x6

		5			4
				2	
	5	6			
1					
2					

Place the numbers 1–6 once in each row, column, and bold-lined jigsaw region composed of six cells.

King's Journey

5	4	3	2	15	16	17
6	7	1	14	20	19	18
8	9	13	21	22	23	24
10	12	37	23	34	26	25
11		48	49			
	41		44	31		

Deduce the journey of a chess king as it visits each square of the grid exactly once, starting at 1 and ending at 49. The king may move one square at a time in any direction, including diagonally.

Dominoes

6	0	0	4	0	1	3	0
4	3	2	1	6	3	5	2
0	2	2	2	5	5	3	6
6	5	4	0	0	5	6	4
1	0	5	3	6	2	1	3
4	1	5	2	6	2	1	3
1	3	4	5	6	1	4	4

Place a full set of regular dominoes into this grid, where 0 represents a blank. Use the chart alongside to tick off the dominoes you've already placed. Each domino is used once only.

0	1	2	3	4	5	6	
							0
							1
							2
							3
							4
							5
							6

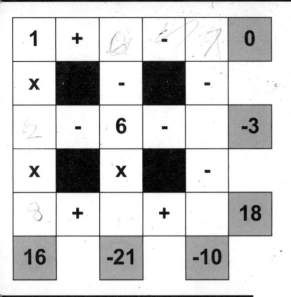

Enter the remaining numbers from 1–9 once in each of the empty squares to complete the sums correctly. Perform calculations from left to right and from top to bottom.

Symbol Values

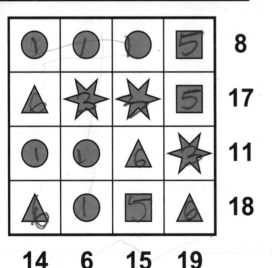

Each of the four shapes represents a positive whole number. The sum of the shapes in each row and column is displayed at the end of each row and column. Using this information can you work out the numerical value of each shape?

Scales

One diamond weighs the same as four squares. Two squares weigh the same as one triangle, while one triangle weighs the same as six stars.

Given this:

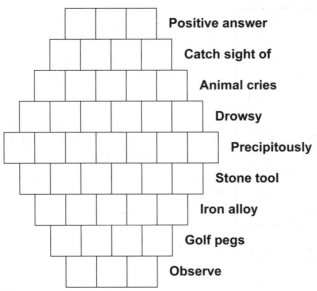

1 How many stars balance with two diamonds?

2 How many triangles balance with three diamonds?

3 If four squares and one diamond are placed on the left side of the scales, how many triangles must be placed on the right side to balance the scales?

Word Egg

Positive answer

Catch sight of

Animal cries

Drowsy

Precipitously

Stone tool

Iron alloy

Golf pegs

Observe

Crack this word egg by answering the clue to the right of each row. Each answer is an anagram of the row above with either one extra or one less letter.

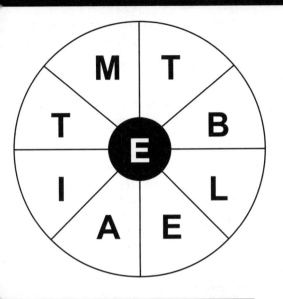

How many words of three or more letters can you find in this wordwheel? Form words by using the letter in the center of the wheel plus a selection from the outer wheel, where no letter may be used more than once in any word.

There is at least one nine-letter word to be found.

Word Pyramid

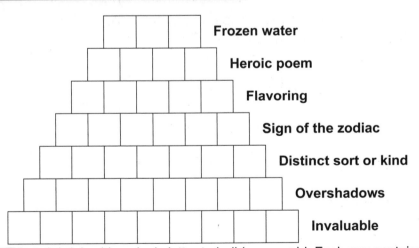

Frozen water

Heroic poem

Flavoring

Sign of the zodiac

Distinct sort or kind

Overshadows

Invaluable

Fill each brick with a single letter to build a pyramid. Each row contains the same bricks as the row beneath but with one missing—however the order may vary. Each row must spell out a word that matches its clue.

63

Knight's Tour

8					
			12	19	30
	7	36	1		
25	22			29	
			27		15
		5	34	17	

The grid represents the moves of a chess knight as it visits each square exactly once, starting at 1 and ending at 36. Work out the rest of the path of the knight and enter the relevant number in each empty cell of the grid. The knight moves either two squares horizontally followed by one square vertically, or two squares vertically followed by one square horizontally.

Word Definer

Can you choose the correct meaning of the following word from the options underneath?

BOTRYOIDAL

1 Shaped like a bunch of grapes

2 Obsessed with perfection

3 Short-lived

ABCDoku

2			3	5
A				
E	D		1	2
1	C	A4	2	

Each square contains a letter and a number. Place 1–5 and A–E once in each row and column to fill the grid. Each combination from A1 through to E5 also appears exactly once in the puzzle.

Binary Puzzle

0				0			
	1		0				1
			0	1			
	0						
	0			0			
		1					
0	0				0		

Fill the grid with 0s and 1s such that 0 and 1 each occur four times in each row and column. The same digit cannot occur in more than two consecutive cells either horizontally or vertically. No whole row can repeat the same series of 0s and 1s as any other row, and no whole column can repeat the same series of 0s and 1s as any other column.

65

Kakuro

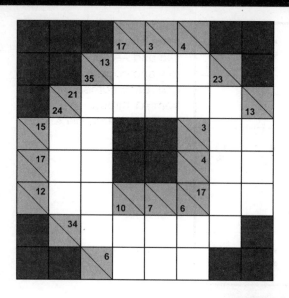

Fill the white squares so that the total in each across or down run of cells matches the total at the start of that run. You must use the numbers from 1–9 only and cannot repeat a number in a run.

Killer 6x6

9		9			12
11			4	10	
6	4	11			
			7		3
9		9		10	
6		6			

Place the numbers 1–6 exactly once per row, column, and 3 x 2 bold-lined box. Additionally the sum total of the squares in each dashed-line shape must match the total given in that shape, and you may not repeat a number within a dashed-line shape.

Word Ladder

LEAF

FALL

Can you climb the rungs of this word ladder? Change only one letter at each step in order to move from the bottom to the top, and do not rearrange the order of the letters.

Pathfinder

R	C	O	I	G	O	L	I	L
E	E	D	C	A	K	E	K	L
D	W	O	P	W	E	H	H	E
N	I	R	R	A	Y	R	C	R
H	F	D	O	B	E	A	U	S
T	D	M	E	L	S	D	D	O
A	O	T	T	O	D	R	O	K
P	O	N	O	D	O	T	W	U
S	E	I	M	U	Y	S	A	M

Moving from letter to adjacent letter, can you find a path that visits every square and spells out the names of several **puzzles**? Start on the shaded square.

Find The Sum

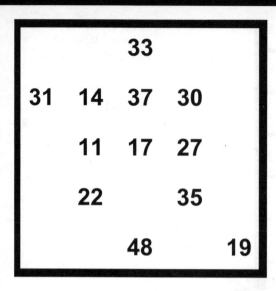

Three of the numbers in this box add up to 113. But can you work out what those three numbers are?

Find The Mines

			3			2	
2		2		4			1
				3		2	
		2		2		1	
2				2			
			2	2		1	0
	1	0				1	
					2		

Find all the mines in the grid. Numbers in certain squares indicate how many mines there are in the neighboring squares, including diagonally touching squares. Mines cannot be placed in squares with numbers.

Hidden Words

Can you find the animals hidden in the sentences below?

1 CEO distraught after losing prize braces in a fire.

2 Writer saw co-author seeking inspiration to overcome writer's block.

Battleships

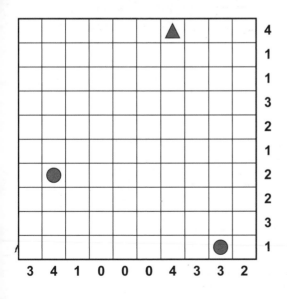

3 4 1 0 0 0 4 3 3 2

4
1
1
3
2
1
2
2
3
1

Locate the position of each of the ships listed below. Numbers around the edge tell you the number of ship segments in each row and column of the puzzle. Ships are surrounded on all sides by water, including diagonally.

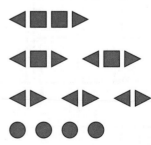

Number Square

1	-	9	x		-21
-		-		+	
	-		-		1
+		+		+	
8	-	2	x	4	24
9		10		14	

Enter the remaining numbers from 1–9 once in each of the empty squares to complete the sums correctly. Perform calculations from left to right and from top to bottom.

Calcudoku

9x		36x	2÷		20x
13+			11+		
			5÷		1÷
	20x		7+		
2-				1-	
11+		3-			

Place the numbers from 1–6 once in each row and column, obeying the sums in the bold-lined regions. Numbers may repeat within the bold-lined regions. With subtraction always take the lower numbers away from the highest number in a region, and with division divide the highest number by the lower numbers.

Binary Puzzle

					0		
			1				1
	0						1
				0	0		
1	0						
		1			0		
				0	0		
1	0		1			0	

Fill the grid with 0s and 1s such that 0 and 1 each occur four times in each row and column. The same digit cannot occur in more than two consecutive cells either horizontally or vertically. No whole row can repeat the same series of 0s and 1s as any other row, and no whole column can repeat the same series of 0s and 1s as any other column.

Symbol Values

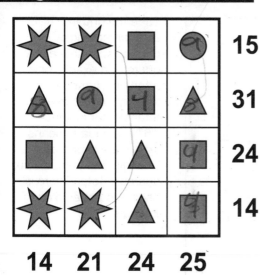

✶	✶	■	●	15
▲	●	■	▲	31
■	▲	▲	■	24
✶	✶	▲	■	14

14 21 24 25

Each of the four shapes represents a positive whole number. The sum of the shapes in each row and column is displayed at the end of each row and column. Using this information can you work out the numerical value of each shape?

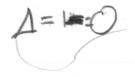

71

Snakeword

Can you find the nine-letter snakeword hidden in this grid? The nine letters form a continuous line passing through each cell once without crossing itself.

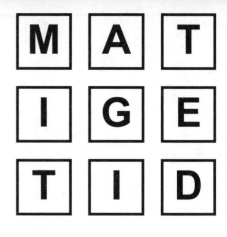

Sikaku

			6				
12				9			
							4
	6						
					8	4	
2		3		3			
			5				
		20			4	4	
			2				
						2	6

Divide the grid into a series of rectangles or squares, such that every square is in exactly one rectangle. Numbers indicate the size of each rectangle: for instance a "6" in a square means that square is part of a rectangle that contains six squares in total. There is only one number in each rectangle.

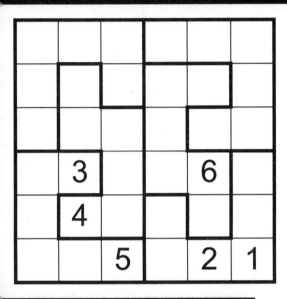

Place the numbers 1–6 once in each row, column, and bold-lined jigsaw region composed of six cells.

Wordwheel

How many words of three or more letters can you find in this wordwheel? Form words by using the letter in the center of the wheel plus a selection from the outer wheel, where no letter may be used more than once in any word.

There is at least one nine-letter word to be found.

Fillomino

Fill every empty square with a number of any value. Each number must form part of a continuous region of squares of size specified by the number. Two different regions with the same number of squares cannot touch horizontally/vertically. Some regions may have no preprinted numbers at all, while others may have multiple preprinted numbers.

2			1		
	1				
3	5		1	7	
	7	5		3	6
				6	
		7			6

Futoshiki

Place the numbers 1–5 exactly once in each row and column. The greater than and less than signs (">" and "<" respectively) indicate where one cell is greater/less than the adjacent cell.

74

Word Scramble

Can you rearrange each of these phrases to make a single word?

1 Retry trio

2 Ten men rap

3 No tin cent

Knight's Tour

	14				12
26		22		34	1
15	24				
4		33	8	31
	36	29		19	
					7

The grid represents the moves of a chess knight as it visits each square exactly once, starting at 1 and ending at 36. Work out the rest of the path of the knight and enter the relevant number in each empty cell of the grid. The knight moves either two squares horizontally followed by one square vertically, or two squares vertically followed by one square horizontally.

75

Word Square

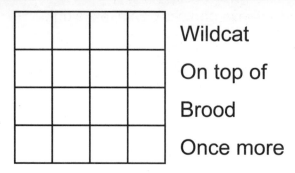

Wildcat

On top of

Brood

Once more

Place four four-letter words to solve each clue such that the words are spelled out both across and down in each of the four rows and columns.

Diamond 24

The sum of the six triangles that compose each hexagon is 24. Can you place numbers from 1–9 in each empty triangle to complete the puzzle? You cannot repeat a number within a hexagon.

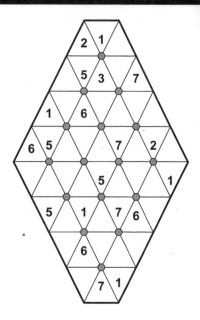

One star weighs the same as two diamonds. Three diamonds weigh the same as one triangle, while one triangle weighs the same as four squares.

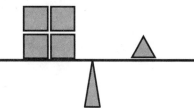

Given this:

1 How many stars balance with two triangles?

2 How many squares balance with six diamonds?

3 Four triangles are placed on the left side of the scales. How many diamonds need to be placed on the right side to balance the scales?

Binary Puzzle

				1	1	
0						
	1			1	1	
				1	1	
	1					0
		1			1	
	0			0		
0		1	1			

Fill the grid with 0s and 1s such that 0 and 1 each occur four times in each row and column. The same digit cannot occur in more than two consecutive cells either horizontally or vertically. No whole row can repeat the same series of 0s and 1s as any other row, and no whole column can repeat the same series of 0s and 1s as any other column.

77

Number Square

	x		x	4	**140**
+	■	x	■	-	
	+	3	x		**81**
-	■	-	■	-	
	+		÷		**10**
5		**13**		**-6**	

Enter the remaining numbers from 1–9 once in each of the empty squares to complete the sums correctly. Perform calculations from left to right and from top to bottom.

Number Tower

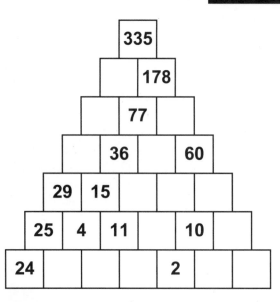

Fill the tower so that every square contains a number. The value of each square in the number tower is the sum of the two squares directly under it.

78

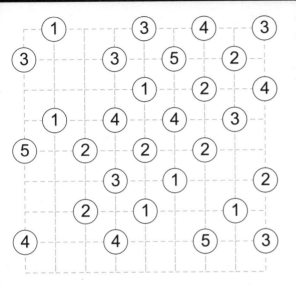

Connect all the circles (which represent islands) into a single interconnected group. The number in a circle represents the number of bridges that connect that island to other islands. Bridges can only be created horizontally or vertically, with no more than two bridges between any pair of islands. Bridges cannot cross any other bridges.

Killer 6x6

3		12			12
7	10	5	11		
			4		
12	9			9	6
	5	7			
			14		

Place the numbers 1–6 exactly once per row, column, and 3 x 2 bold-lined box. Additionally the sum total of the squares in each dashed-line shape must match the total given in that shape, and you may not repeat a number within a dashed-line shape.

ABCDoku

				2
5		B	E	A1
	D			B
E			4	C
		2		

Each square contains a letter and a number. Place 1–5 and A–E once in each row and column to fill the grid. Each combination from A1 through to E5 also appears exactly once in the puzzle.

King's Journey

			8			
		15		7	6	
13			32		34	1
19				38		
20			40	47		
23		29		49	48	45
	25	27				

Deduce the journey of a chess king as it visits each square of the grid exactly once, starting at 1 and ending at 49. The king may move one square at a time in any direction, including diagonally.

80

GONE

cone

cane

cart

PAST

Can you climb the rungs of this word ladder? Change only one letter at each step in order to move from the bottom to the top, and do not rearrange the order of the letters.

Snakeword

Can you find the nine-letter snakeword hidden in this grid? The nine letters form a continuous line passing through each cell once without crossing itself.

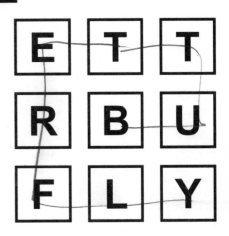

Jigsaw 6x6

			3	2	
	4			6	
		2			
4					
				1	
		1			

Place the numbers 1–6 once in each row, column, and bold-lined jigsaw region composed of six cells.

Find The Mines

				1		2	
0		3					
	2		2	1	2		2
1					1		
			1			3	
	2						1
	2				2		
		2		1		2	

Find all the mines in the grid. Numbers in certain squares indicate how many mines there are in the neighboring squares, including diagonally touching squares. Mines cannot be placed in squares with numbers.

82

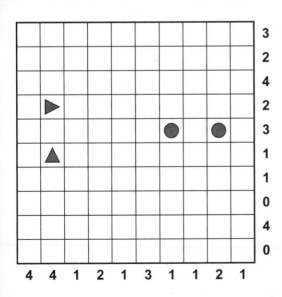

Divide the grid into a series of rectangles, such that every square is in exactly one rectangle. Numbers indicate the size of each rectangle: for instance a "6" in a square means that square is part of a rectangle that contains six squares in total. There is only one number in each rectangle.

Battleships

Locate the position of each of the ships listed below. Numbers around the edge tell you the number of ship segments in each row and column of the puzzle. Ships are surrounded on all sides by water, including diagonally.

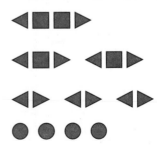

Kakuro

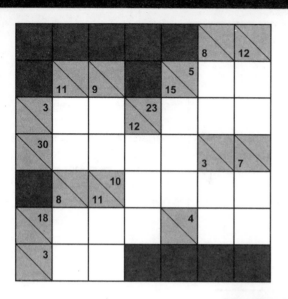

Fill the white squares so that the total in each across or down run of cells matches the total at the start of that run. You must use the numbers from 1–9 only and cannot repeat a number in a run.

Killer 6x6

Place the numbers 1–6 exactly once per row, column, and 3 x 2 bold-lined box. Additionally the sum total of the squares in each dashed-line shape must match the total given in that shape, and you may not repeat a number within a dashed-line shape.

5		13			7
10	11		8		
		7			3
6	14			6	
	13	4	5		14

Hidden Words

Can you find the signs of the zodiac hidden in the sentences below?

1 The decorator decided on a beige minimalist color scheme for the room.

2 Recently some chili brands were told off for making peppers that were too hot to eat.

Pathfinder

L	D	H	G	N	I	R	E	T
E	D	U	O	N	Y	O	U	T
R	N	Y	L	C	K	B	Q	A
E	A	C	O	A	R	T	U	H
A	P	M	M	P	I	E	E	C
M	C	O	A	E	B	L	T	H
R	M	T	E	C	R	G	G	C
A	Y	R	T	A	O	G	A	N
W	S	E	T	B	W	D	B	U

Moving from letter to adjacent letter, can you find a path that visits every square and spells out the names of several **collective terms**? Start on the shaded square.

Number Tower

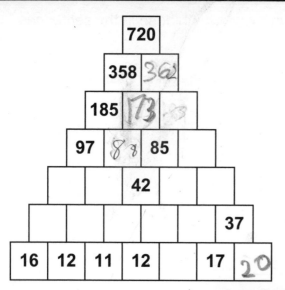

Fill the tower so that every square contains a number. The value of each square in the number tower is the sum of the two squares directly under it.

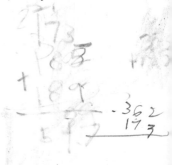

Word Square

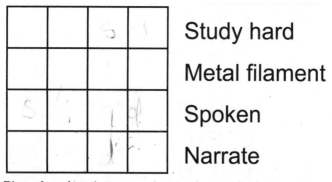

Study hard

Metal filament

Spoken

Narrate

Place four four-letter words to solve each clue such that the words are spelled out both across and down in each of the four rows and columns.

Bridges

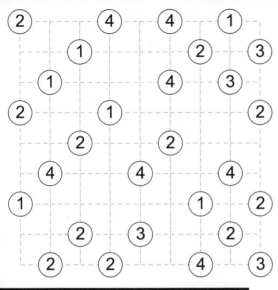

Connect all the circles (which represent islands) into a single interconnected group. The number in a circle represents the number of bridges that connect that island to other islands. Bridges can only be created horizontally or vertically, with no more than two bridges between any pair of islands. Bridges cannot cross any other bridges.

Calcudoku

3÷		12+	10+		20x
6x					
7+	12x			7+	
	120x			18x	
15x		1-	1-	10+	
10+					

Place the numbers from 1–6 once in each row and column, obeying the sums in the bold-lined regions. Numbers may repeat within the bold-lined regions. With subtraction always take the lower numbers away from the highest number in a region, and with division divide the highest number by the lower numbers.

87

Word Scramble

Can you rearrange each of these phrases to make a single word?

1 Oh gray peg

2 Tired moon

3 No exec tip

Futoshiki

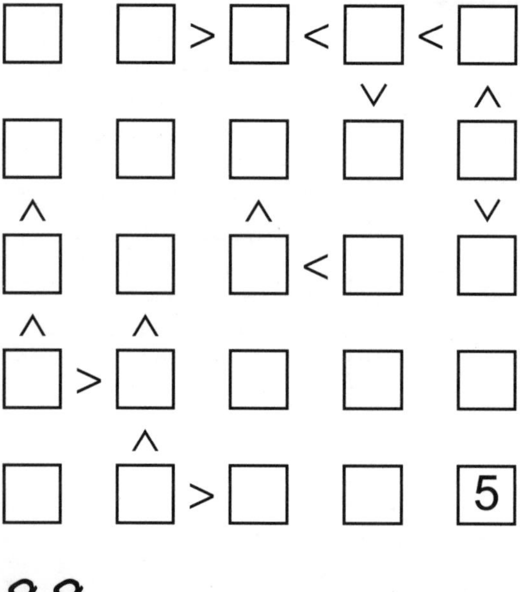

Place the numbers 1–5 exactly once in each row and column. The greater than and less than signs (">" and "<" respectively) indicate where one cell is greater/less than the adjacent cell.

Binary Puzzle

Fill the grid with 0s and 1s such that 0 and 1 each occur four times in each row and column. The same digit cannot occur in more than two consecutive cells either horizontally or vertically. No whole row can repeat the same series of 0s and 1s as any other row, and no whole column can repeat the same series of 0s and 1s as any other column.

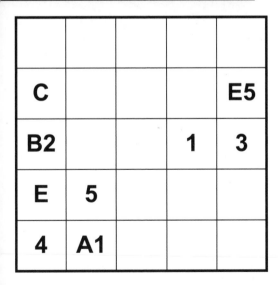

ABCDoku

Each square contains a letter and a number. Place 1–5 and A–E once in each row and column to fill the grid. Each combination from A1 through to E5 also appears exactly once in the puzzle.

Kakuro

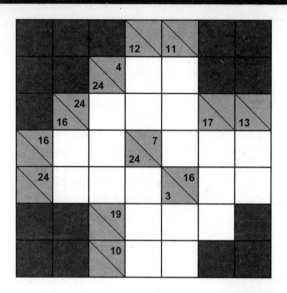

Fill the white squares so that the total in each across or down run of cells matches the total at the start of that run. You must use the numbers from 1–9 only and cannot repeat a number in a run.

Diamond 25

The sum of the six triangles that compose each hexagon is 25. Can you place numbers from 1–9 in each empty triangle to complete the puzzle? You cannot repeat a number within a hexagon.

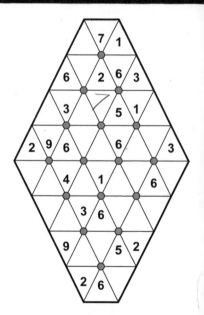

Fillomino

Fill every empty square with a number of any value. Each number must form part of a continuous region of squares of size specified by the number. Two different regions with the same number of squares cannot touch horizontally/vertically. Some regions may have no preprinted numbers at all, while others may have multiple preprinted numbers.

	4		4		
		5			
1	3		5	7	
	7	5		1	2
			1		
		1		4	

Find The Mines

1							1
		2	2		2	2	
2						1	
		0		2			
				3			1
	2				2		2
1			3		1	2	
	1				1		2

Find all the mines in the grid. Numbers in certain squares indicate how many mines there are in the neighboring squares, including diagonally touching squares. Mines cannot be placed in squares with numbers.

ABCDoku

			3	C
C5		D		E
	2			A
1	3			
			A	

Each square contains a letter and a number. Place 1–5 and A–E once in each row and column to fill the grid. Each combination from A1 through to E5 also appears exactly once in the puzzle.

Battleships

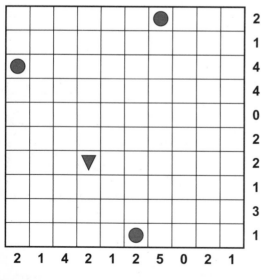

Locate the position of each of the ships listed below. Numbers around the edge tell you the number of ship segments in each row and column of the puzzle. Ships are surrounded on all sides by water, including diagonally.

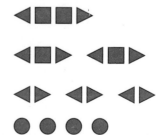

92

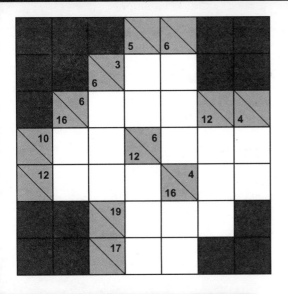

Fill the white squares so that the total in each across or down run of cells matches the total at the start of that run. You must use the numbers from 1–9 only and cannot repeat a number in a run.

Snakeword

Can you find the nine-letter snakeword hidden in this grid? The nine letters form a continuous line passing through each cell once without crossing itself.

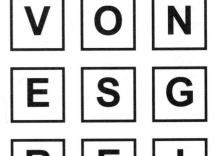

Word Square

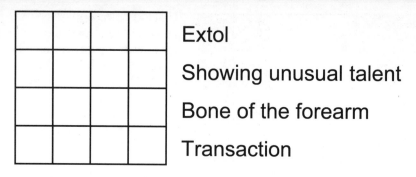

Extol

Showing unusual talent

Bone of the forearm

Transaction

Place four four-letter words to solve each clue such that the words are spelled out both across and down in each of the four rows and columns.

Diamond 24

The sum of the six triangles that compose each hexagon is 24. Can you place numbers from 1–9 in each empty triangle to complete the puzzle? You cannot repeat a number within a hexagon.

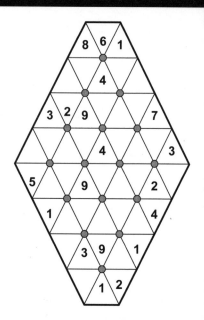

Dominoes

4	0	2	2	1	0	5	3
4	3	6	4	5	5	0	6
6	6	2	2	4	4	1	3
4	6	0	4	3	6	5	2
0	2	0	5	1	3	3	1
6	2	6	3	5	3	2	5
4	1	1	0	5	0	1	1

Place a full set of regular dominoes into this grid, where 0 represents a blank. Use the chart alongside to tick off the dominoes you've already placed. Each domino is used once only.

0	1	2	3	4	5	6	
							0
							1
							2
							3
							4
							5
							6

Futoshiki

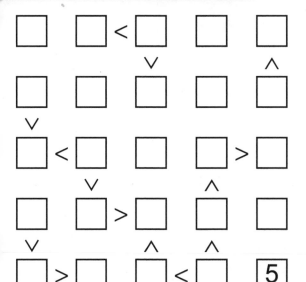

Place the numbers 1–5 exactly once in each row and column. The greater than and less than signs (">" and "<" respectively) indicate where one cell is greater/less than the adjacent cell.

Knight's Tour

	6	27			
	17		7		11
	32	*5*	28		36
		16	1	*8*	21
	4	*9*		35	2
24			*3*	22	13

The grid represents the moves of a chess knight as it visits each square exactly once, starting at 1 and ending at 36. Work out the rest of the path of the knight and enter the relevant number in each empty cell of the grid. The knight moves either two squares horizontally followed by one square vertically, or two squares vertically followed by one square horizontally.

Pathfinder

D	K	A	K	N	I	P	A	R
O	R	O	G	N	D	Y	M	T
V	A	N	I	A	A	T	I	I
T	E	G	N	R	B	A	R	N
N	S	E	B	L	R	G	L	I
U	R	K	C	A	A	M	E	M
S	U	S	S	I	A	E	M	O
A	U	Q	I	D	N	L	I	N
L	I	E	T	R	A	C	A	B

Moving from letter to adjacent letter, can you find a path that visits every square and spells out the names of several **cocktails and garnishes**? Start on the shaded square.

96

Sikaku grid (top):

Row 1: (col6) 4, (col7) 2, (col8) 2, (col9) 2
Row 2: (col1) 4, (col6) 4
Row 3: (col3) 12, (col4) 2, (col7) 3
Row 4: (col4) 2
Row 5: (col9) 18
Row 6: (col2) 2, (col4) 10
Row 7: (col1) 6, (col2) 2, (col5) 12
Row 8: (col2) 3
Row 9:
Row 10: (col2) 3, (col5) 3, (col9) 4

Divide the grid into a series of rectangles or squares, such that every square is in exactly one rectangle. Numbers indicate the size of each rectangle: for instance a "6" in a square means that square is part of a rectangle that contains six squares in total. There is only one number in each rectangle.

Killer 6x6

Killer 6x6 grid:

Row 1: 10, 7, 8
Row 2: 8, 14, 6
Row 3: 7, 11
Row 4: 12, 8, 4
Row 5: 10, 9
Row 6: 3, 9

Place the numbers 1–6 exactly once per row, column, and 3 x 2 bold-lined box. Additionally the sum total of the squares in each dashed-line shape must match the total given in that shape, and you may not repeat a number within a dashed-line shape.

97

Number Tower

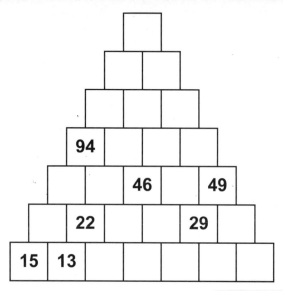

Fill the tower so that every square contains a number. The value of each square in the number tower is the sum of the two squares directly under it.

Word Ladder

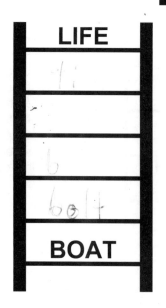

Can you climb the rungs of this word ladder? Change only one letter at each step in order to move from the bottom to the top, and do not rearrange the order of the letters.

Symbol Values

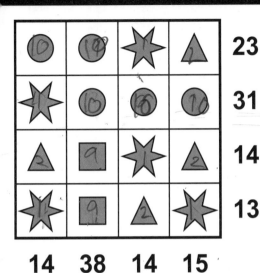

⊙	⊙	✶	△	**23**
✶	⊙	⊙	⊙	**31**
△	▢	✶	△	**14**
✶	▢	△	✶	**13**
14	**38**	**14**	**15**	

Each of the four shapes represents a positive whole number. The sum of the shapes in each row and column is displayed at the end of each row and column. Using this information can you work out the numerical value of each shape?

Word Egg

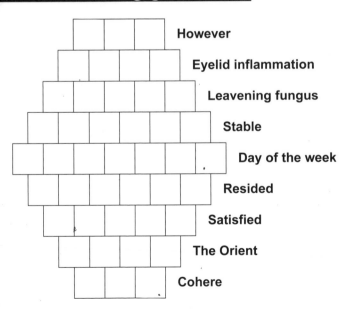

However

Eyelid inflammation

Leavening fungus

Stable

Day of the week

Resided

Satisfied

The Orient

Cohere

Crack this word egg by answering the clue to the right of each row. Each answer is an anagram of the row above with either one extra or one less letter.

Word Definer

Can you choose the correct meaning of the following word from the options underneath?

INVEIGLE

1 Vain

2 Entice

3 Procrastinate

Wordwheel

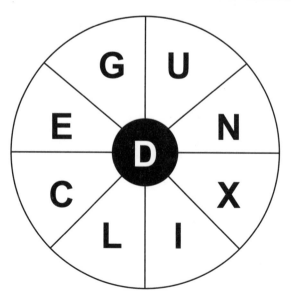

How many words of three or more letters can you find in this wordwheel? Form words by using the letter in the center of the wheel plus a selection from the outer wheel, where no letter may be used more than once in any word.

There is at least one nine-letter word to be found.

Word Scramble

Can you rearrange each of these phrases to make a single word?

1 Sense rage

2 Oar timing

3 Dries cane

Find The Sum

12	34	29	
	38		26
33	13	36	18
			30
	19	39	

Three of the numbers in this box add up to 109. But can you work out what those three numbers are?

ABC Logic

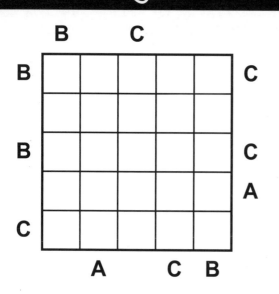

Place the letters A, B, and C exactly once in each row and column. Each row and column has two blank cells. The letters at the edge of a row/column indicate which of the letters is the first/last to appear in that row/column.

Binary Puzzle

		1			0	
0				0	0	
			1			
		1			1	
			0			0
	0		0		0	
1						
0			0			

Fill the grid with 0s and 1s such that 0 and 1 each occur four times in each row and column. The same digit cannot occur in more than two consecutive cells either horizontally or vertically. No whole row can repeat the same series of 0s and 1s as any other row, and no whole column can repeat the same series of 0s and 1s as any other column.

9+	14+			24x	7+
		30x			
3÷			40x		
6x		6x			15x
11+	10+			1÷	
		5÷			

Place the numbers from 1–6 once in each row and column, obeying the sums in the bold-lined regions. Numbers may repeat within the bold-lined regions. With subtraction always take the lower numbers away from the highest number in a region, and with division divide the highest number by the lower numbers.

Jigsaw 6x6

3			4		
6		5		3	
4					
	1				2

Place the numbers 1–6 once in each row, column, and bold-lined jigsaw region composed of six cells.

King's Journey

	25			21	1	
		30	31			
28	39			32		4
	41		36		18	
			37		12	
47	48	45				
49		15		10		

Deduce the journey of a chess king as it visits each square of the grid exactly once, starting at 1 and ending at 49. The king may move one square at a time in any direction, including diagonally.

Dominoes

4	6	0	3	5	3	6	1
5	4	5	4	2	2	5	4
1	4	0	2	0	4	6	6
1	1	6	1	2	4	5	2
4	2	3	3	2	1	0	6
0	0	2	0	6	6	5	5
1	3	3	3	3	1	0	5

Place a full set of regular dominoes into this grid, where 0 represents a blank. Use the chart alongside to tick off the dominoes you've already placed. Each domino is used once only.

0	1	2	3	4	5	6	
							0
							1
							2
							3
							4
							5
							6

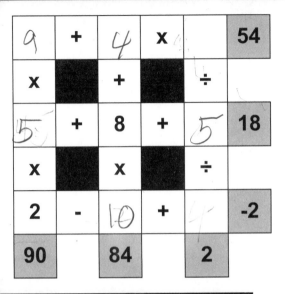

Enter the remaining numbers from 1–9 once in each of the empty squares to complete the sums correctly. Perform calculations from left to right and from top to bottom.

Symbol Values

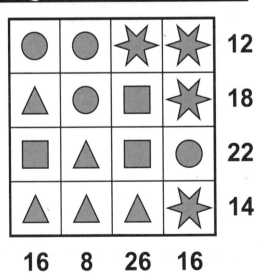

Each of the four shapes represents a positive whole number. The sum of the shapes in each row and column is displayed at the end of each row and column. Using this information can you work out the numerical value of each shape?

105

Scales

Two diamonds weigh the same as four circles. One circle weighs the same as two squares, while one square is half the weight of one triangle.

Given this:

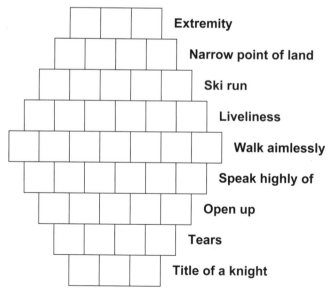

1 How many diamonds balance with four triangles?

2 How many squares balance with three diamonds?

3 If there are two triangles, one diamond, and four squares on the left side of the scales, how many circles must be placed on the right side of the scales in order for them to balance?

Word Egg

Extremity

Narrow point of land

Ski run

Liveliness

Walk aimlessly

Speak highly of

Open up

Tears

Title of a knight

Crack this word egg by answering the clue to the right of each row. Each answer is an anagram of the row above with either one extra or one less letter.

How many words of three or more letters can you find in this wordwheel? Form words by using the letter in the center of the wheel plus a selection from the outer wheel, where no letter may be used more than once in any word.

There is at least one nine-letter word to be found.

Word Pyramid

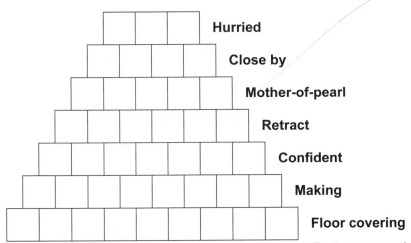

Hurried

Close by

Mother-of-pearl

Retract

Confident

Making

Floor covering

Fill each brick with a single letter to build a pyramid. Each row contains the same bricks as the row beneath but with one missing—however the order may vary. Each row must spell out a word that matches its clue.

Knight's Tour

24 31	4	15	18	29	
5	16	25 30	3	14	
34	23 32	17	28 19		
9	6 35	26	13	2	
22	33	8	11	20	27
7	10 21	36	1	12	

The grid represents the moves of a chess knight as it visits each square exactly once, starting at 1 and ending at 36. Work out the rest of the path of the knight and enter the relevant number in each empty cell of the grid. The knight moves either two squares horizontally followed by one square vertically, or two squares vertically followed by one square horizontally.

Word Definer

Can you choose the correct meaning of the following word from the options underneath?

SOUGH

1 A constellation

2 A farm implement

3 Make a rushing sound

ABCDoku

			D	1
	C	2	A	
	E	A1		
C3			5	

Each square contains a letter and a number. Place 1–5 and A–E once in each row and column to fill the grid. Each combination from A1 through to E5 also appears exactly once in the puzzle.

Binary Puzzle

1		1			1		
	0						
			1				1
	1	1					1
			1				
		0		0		1	0
0	0				0		
1							

Fill the grid with 0s and 1s such that 0 and 1 each occur four times in each row and column. The same digit cannot occur in more than two consecutive cells either horizontally or vertically. No whole row can repeat the same series of 0s and 1s as any other row, and no whole column can repeat the same series of 0s and 1s as any other column.

Kakuro

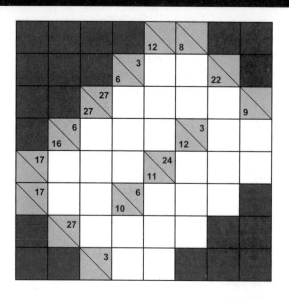

Fill the white squares so that the total in each across or down run of cells matches the total at the start of that run. You must use the numbers from 1–9 only and cannot repeat a number in a run.

Killer 6x6

10	10		8		
	3	5	9	9	12
10	12				
	13			4	
6			15		

Place the numbers 1–6 exactly once per row, column, and 3 x 2 bold-lined box. Additionally the sum total of the squares in each dashed-line shape must match the total given in that shape, and you may not repeat a number within a dashed-line shape.

Word Ladder

NEON

neon

moon

mood

mold

GOLD

Can you climb the rungs of this word ladder? Change only one letter at each step in order to move from the bottom to the top, and do not rearrange the order of the letters.

Pathfinder

O	R	T	E	R	A	G	M	A
B	E	R	C	H	A	R	A	I
Z	I	T	I	M	E	L	I	C
A	L	E	E	S	O	J	R	T
B	E	A	M	E	S	S	U	A
H	T	J	H	P	R	D	S	P
C	H	Y	R	I	A	N	A	S
R	A	H	T	C	H	T	H	A
L	E	S	O	R	O	D	O	M

Moving from letter to adjacent letter, can you find a path that visits every square and spells out several **names**? Start on the shaded square.

Find The Sum

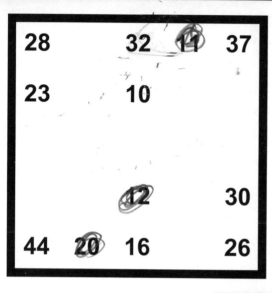

28	32	11	37
23	10		
		12	30
44	20	16	26

Three of the numbers in this box add up to 43. But can you work out what those three numbers are?

Find The Mines

	1				2		
2		3		4		1	
2						1	
2			2	3		2	
				2			
		2		2	3	4	
1	1	1					
	1		1		2		2

Find all the mines in the grid. Numbers in certain squares indicate how many mines there are in the neighboring squares, including diagonally touching squares. Mines cannot be placed in squares with numbers.

112

Hidden Words

Can you find the fruits hidden in the sentences below?

1 The oystercatcher Ryan saw was well worth the wait, with its impressive brightly colored bill.

2 The painter received many accolades for a truly wonderful landscape artwork.

Battleships

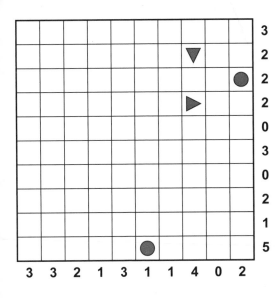

										3
							▼			2
								●		2
							▶			2
										0
										3
										0
										2
										1
				●						5
3	3	2	1	3	1	1	4	0	2	

Locate the position of each of the ships listed below. Numbers around the edge tell you the number of ship segments in each row and column of the puzzle. Ships are surrounded on all sides by water, including diagonally.

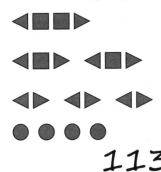

113

Number Square

	+		**x**		**90**
-	■	**x**	■	**x**	
	x		**+**		**23**
+	■	**+**	■		**-**
1	**-**		**-**	**3**	**-6**
0		**18**		**27**	

Enter the remaining numbers from 1–9 once in each of the empty squares to complete the sums correctly. Perform calculations from left to right and from top to bottom.

Calcudoku

7+		11+			8+
1÷			14+		
20x		9+			12+
1÷					
7+		9+			4-
	5x		24x		

Place the numbers from 1–6 once in each row and column, obeying the sums in the bold-lined regions. Numbers may repeat within the bold-lined regions. With subtraction always take the lower numbers away from the highest number in a region, and with division divide the highest number by the lower numbers.

Binary Puzzle

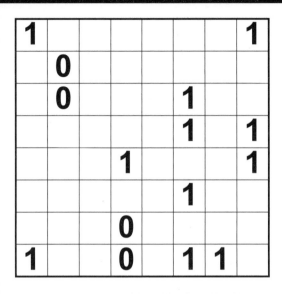

Fill the grid with 0s and 1s such that 0 and 1 each occur four times in each row and column. The same digit cannot occur in more than two consecutive cells either horizontally or vertically. No whole row can repeat the same series of 0s and 1s as any other row, and no whole column can repeat the same series of 0s and 1s as any other column.

Symbol Values

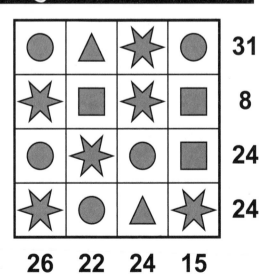

Each of the four shapes represents a positive whole number. The sum of the shapes in each row and column is displayed at the end of each row and column. Using this information can you work out the numerical value of each shape?

N

Snakeword

Can you find the nine-letter snakeword hidden in this grid? The nine letters form a continuous line passing through each cell once without crossing itself.

Sikaku

4	2			4	3		
	2						
4					9		
	8					12	
	8	10					2
			9				
		4					3
	2					3	
	2	4				5	

Divide the grid into a series of rectangles or squares, such that every square is in exactly one rectangle. Numbers indicate the size of each rectangle: for instance a "6" in a square means that square is part of a rectangle that contains six squares in total. There is only one number in each rectangle.

Place the numbers 1–6 once in each row, column, and bold-lined jigsaw region composed of six cells.

				5	
				4	
	5	3			
2					
	6	5			

Wordwheel

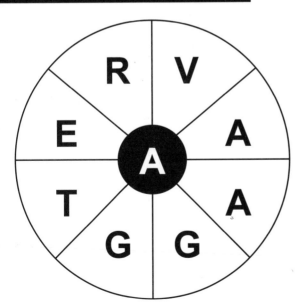

How many words of three or more letters can you find in this wordwheel? Form words by using the letter in the center of the wheel plus a selection from the outer wheel, where no letter may be used more than once in any word.

There is at least one nine-letter word to be found.

Fillomino

Fill every empty square with a number of any value. Each number must form part of a continuous region of squares of size specified by the number. Two different regions with the same number of squares cannot touch horizontally/vertically. Some regions may have no preprinted numbers at all, while others may have multiple preprinted numbers.

	6	6	7		
	2	1		5	5
1	2		2	5	
		3	6	2	

Futoshiki

Place the numbers 1–5 exactly once in each row and column. The greater than and less than signs (">" and "<" respectively) indicate where one cell is greater/less than the adjacent cell.

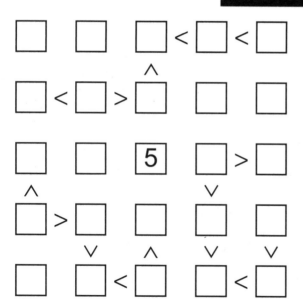

118

Can you rearrange each of these phrases to make a single word?

1 Recap life

2 Thy chain

3 Dimes I dug

Knight's Tour

30	15	20	**7**	28	13
19	8	**29**	14	**21**	6
16	31	18	**27**	**12**	35
1	26	9	**36**	5	22
32	17	**24**	3	**34**	11
25	2	**33**	**10**	23	**4**

The grid represents the moves of a chess knight as it visits each square exactly once, starting at 1 and ending at 36. Work out the rest of the path of the knight and enter the relevant number in each empty cell of the grid. The knight moves either two squares horizontally followed by one square vertically, or two squares vertically followed by one square horizontally.

Word Square

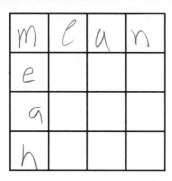

m	e	a	n
e			
a			
h			

Harsh

Capital of Italy

Fairies

Woven fabric

Place four four-letter words to solve each clue such that the words are spelled out both across and down in each of the four rows and columns.

Diamond 26

The sum of the six triangles that compose each hexagon is 26. Can you place numbers from 1–9 in each empty triangle to complete the puzzle? You cannot repeat a number within a hexagon.

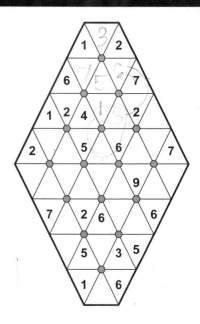

Can you choose the correct meaning of the following word from the options underneath?

ROUNDEL

1 A decorative medallion

2 A type of weighing scale

3 An ancient medicine

Binary Puzzle

		1	1				
1	1			0		0	
	0	0		0			0
1			0				
					0		0
		1				1	
0							

Fill the grid with 0s and 1s such that 0 and 1 each occur four times in each row and column. The same digit cannot occur in more than two consecutive cells either horizontally or vertically. No whole row can repeat the same series of 0s and 1s as any other row, and no whole column can repeat the same series of 0s and 1s as any other column.

Number Square

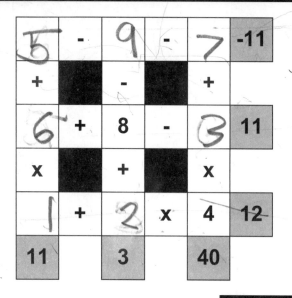

5	-	9	-	7	-11
+		-		+	
6	+	8	-	3	11
x		+		x	
1	+	2	x	4	12
11		3		40	

Enter the remaining numbers from 1–9 once in each of the empty squares to complete the sums correctly. Perform calculations from left to right and from top to bottom.

Number Tower

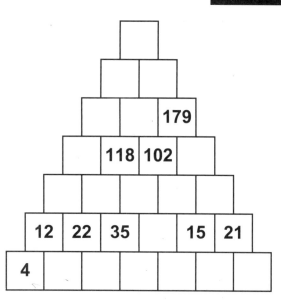

		179			
	118	102			
12	22	35		15	21
4					

Fill the tower so that every square contains a number. The value of each square in the number tower is the sum of the two squares directly under it.

122

Bridges

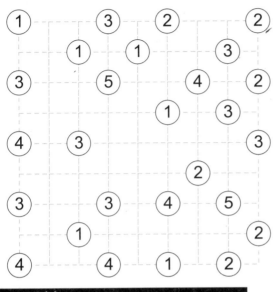

Connect all the circles (which represent islands) into a single interconnected group. The number in a circle represents the number of bridges that connect that island to other islands. Bridges can only be created horizontally or vertically, with no more than two bridges between any pair of islands. Bridges cannot cross any other bridges.

Killer 6x6

9	8	9		8	
			8		
7		12		6	9
7		4			
5			15	8	
11					

Place the numbers 1–6 exactly once per row, column, and 3 x 2 bold-lined box. Additionally the sum total of the squares in each dashed-line shape must match the total given in that shape, and you may not repeat a number within a dashed-line shape.

ABCDoku

		2	E5	A
D				5
	2			B
	4	3		D

Each square contains a letter and a number. Place 1–5 and A–E once in each row and column to fill the grid. Each combination from A1 through to E5 also appears exactly once in the puzzle.

King's Journey

		39				9
43				14	11	
	49			35		
	46	48	36			6
			33	18		
	28				1	
26	25	22	21			2

Deduce the journey of a chess king as it visits each square of the grid exactly once, starting at 1 and ending at 49. The king may move one square at a time in any direction, including diagonally.

124

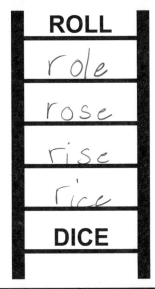

ROLL

role

rose

rise

rice

DICE

Can you climb the rungs of this word ladder? Change only one letter at each step in order to move from the bottom to the top, and do not rearrange the order of the letters.

Snakeword

Can you find the nine-letter snakeword hidden in this grid? The nine letters form a continuous line passing through each cell once without crossing itself.

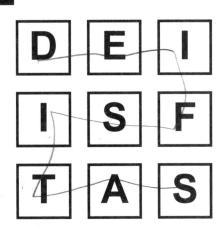

Jigsaw 6x6

		4			3
		1			
2			4		
			2		
			5		1

Place the numbers 1–6 once in each row, column, and bold-lined jigsaw region composed of six cells.

Find The Mines

	2		2		1		1
1				3			
		2	2				2
					5		
	3						
	4			0		1	
			3		1		0
	2		3				

Find all the mines in the grid. Numbers in certain squares indicate how many mines there are in the neighboring squares, including diagonally touching squares. Mines cannot be placed in squares with numbers.

126

4				2			
	8		8		12		
		2	2		4		2
						4	
	2		18				3
	2						
	2					5	
	3		4			3	
		10					

Divide the grid into a series of rectangles, such that every square is in exactly one rectangle. Numbers indicate the size of each rectangle: for instance a "6" in a square means that square is part of a rectangle that contains six squares in total. There is only one number in each rectangle.

Battleships

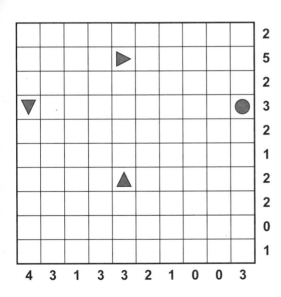

4	3	1	3	3	2	1	0	0	3	

2
5
2
3
2
1
2
2
0
1

Locate the position of each of the ships listed below. Numbers around the edge tell you the number of ship segments in each row and column of the puzzle. Ships are surrounded on all sides by water, including diagonally.

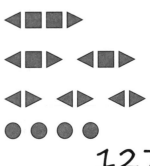

Kakuro

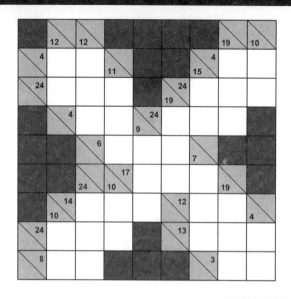

Fill the white squares so that the total in each across or down run of cells matches the total at the start of that run. You must use the numbers from 1–9 only and cannot repeat a number in a run.

Killer 6x6

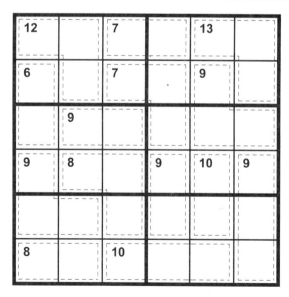

Place the numbers 1–6 exactly once per row, column, and 3 x 2 bold-lined box. Additionally the sum total of the squares in each dashed-line shape must match the total given in that shape, and you may not repeat a number within a dashed-line shape.

Hidden Words

Can you find the family members hidden in the sentences below?

1 Chef sacked for couscous initiative—perhaps that's a bit harsh!

2 The gardener decided to shun clematis in favor of honeysuckle.

Pathfinder

A	G	E	D	Y	L	A	C	S
R	N	O	S	P	U	S	E	E
T	M	V	O	M	A	S	C	N
E	O	N	L	I	M	E	O	I
C	N	E	B	O	O	R	P	R
N	T	U	E	B	A	H	A	S
E	A	G	F	E	L	T	R	A
R	L	R	R	R	P	S	S	H
U	A	A	I	A	E	E	K	A

Moving from letter to adjacent letter, can you find a path that visits every square and spells out several words relating to **Romeo and Juliet**? Start on the shaded square.

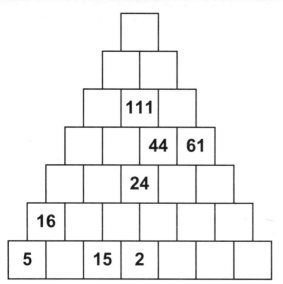

Fill the tower so that every square contains a number. The value of each square in the number tower is the sum of the two squares directly under it.

Word Square

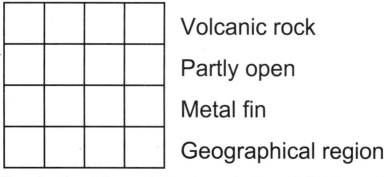

Volcanic rock

Partly open

Metal fin

Geographical region

Place four four-letter words to solve each clue such that the words are spelled out both across and down in each of the four rows and columns.

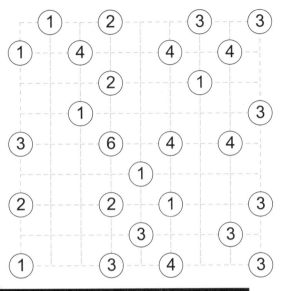

Connect all the circles (which represent islands) into a single interconnected group. The number in a circle represents the number of bridges that connect that island to other islands. Bridges can only be created horizontally or vertically, with no more than two bridges between any pair of islands. Bridges cannot cross any other bridges.

Calcudoku

2-	12+	5+		12+	18x
		90x			
9+					8+
	9+			6x	
5x	11+	5+			
			72x		

Place the numbers from 1–6 once in each row and column, obeying the sums in the bold-lined regions. Numbers may repeat within the bold-lined regions. With subtraction always take the lower numbers away from the highest number in a region, and with division divide the highest number by the lower numbers.

Word Scramble

Can you rearrange each of these phrases to make a single word?

1 Sun overly

2 Lent curry

3 Triple bun

Futoshiki

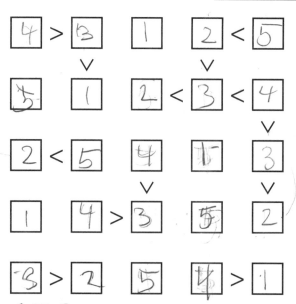

Place the numbers 1–5 exactly once in each row and column. The greater than and less than signs (">" and "<" respectively) indicate where one cell is greater/less than the adjacent cell.

132

Fill the grid with 0s and 1s such that 0 and 1 each occur four times in each row and column. The same digit cannot occur in more than two consecutive cells either horizontally or vertically. No whole row can repeat the same series of 0s and 1s as any other row, and no whole column can repeat the same series of 0s and 1s as any other column.

			1	1			
				1			
1				0	1		
	0				0		0
	1			1			
	1				0		

ABCDoku

Each square contains a letter and a number. Place 1–5 and A–E once in each row and column to fill the grid. Each combination from A1 through to E5 also appears exactly once in the puzzle.

	C			
		E	C1	B
	3		D	
		2		E
1				4

Kakuro

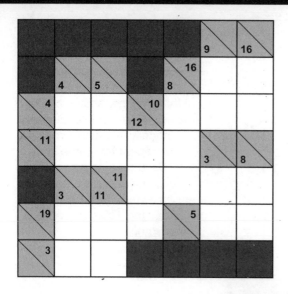

Fill the white squares so that the total in each across or down run of cells matches the total at the start of that run. You must use the numbers from 1–9 only and cannot repeat a number in a run.

The sum of the six triangles that compose each hexagon is 25. Can you place numbers from 1–9 in each empty triangle to complete the puzzle? You cannot repeat a number within a hexagon.

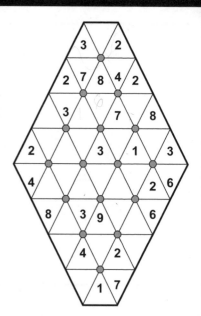

13	2	29	22	11	4
30	21	12	3	28	23
1	14	27	34	5	10
20	31	18	9	24	35
15	8	33	26	17	6
32	19	16	7	36	25

The grid represents the moves of a chess knight as it visits each square exactly once, starting at 1 and ending at 36. Work out the rest of the path of the knight and enter the relevant number in each empty cell of the grid. The knight moves either two squares horizontally followed by one square vertically, or two squares vertically followed by one square horizontally.

Find The Sum

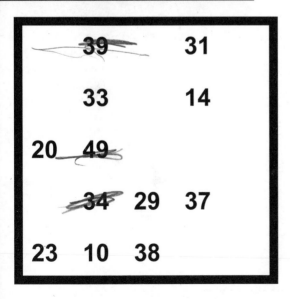

39		31
	33	14
20	49	
	34	29	37
23	10	38

Three of the numbers in this box add up to 122. But can you work out what those three numbers are?

Word Square

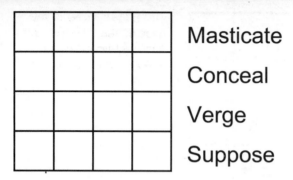

Masticate

Conceal

Verge

Suppose

Place four four-letter words to solve each clue such that the words are spelled out both across and down in each of the four rows and columns.

Sikaku

	2		3			3		
2						2		
	2	2				2		
8			6					
				5	2	2		
	2	2				20		
	2					9		
							20	
		4						

Divide the grid into a series of rectangles or squares, such that every square is in exactly one rectangle. Numbers indicate the size of each rectangle: for instance a "6" in a square means that square is part of a rectangle that contains six squares in total. There is only one number in each rectangle.

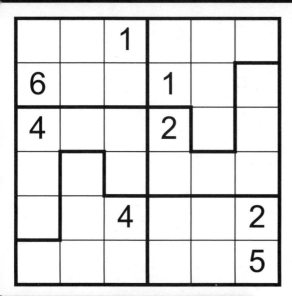

Place the numbers 1–6 once in each row, column, and bold-lined jigsaw region composed of six cells.

Wordwheel

qui

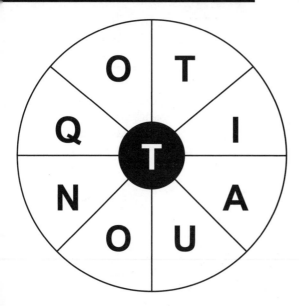

How many words of three or more letters can you find in this wordwheel? Form words by using the letter in the center of the wheel plus a selection from the outer wheel, where no letter may be used more than once in any word.

There is at least one nine-letter word to be found.

Fillomino

Fill every empty square with a number of any value. Each number must form part of a continuous region of squares of size specified by the number. Two different regions with the same number of squares cannot touch horizontally/vertically. Some regions may have no preprinted numbers at all, while others may have multiple preprinted numbers.

8	1		6	2	
	8				
		8		1	
	8		1		
				6	
	3	5		2	6

Futoshiki

Place the numbers 1–5 exactly once in each row and column. The greater than and less than signs (">" and "<" respectively) indicate where one cell is greater/less than the adjacent cell.

☐ ☐ ☐ < ☐ ☐
∧
☐ > ☐ > ☐ ☐ ☐
∧   ∨
☐ ☐ ☐ ☐ > ☐
                          ∧
☐ < ☐ ☐ ☐ ☐
      ∧   ∧
☐ < ☐ > ☐ > ☐ 5

138

Number Square

	x		x		160
+	■	+	■	+	
3	x	1	x		18
-	■	+	■	-	
	x		x		126
6		18		3	

Enter the remaining numbers from 1–9 once in each of the empty squares to complete the sums correctly. Perform calculations from left to right and from top to bottom.

Knight's Tour

7				1	
20					25
9				13	
		30		36	
5	32				14
22	29			16	35

The grid represents the moves of a chess knight as it visits each square exactly once, starting at 1 and ending at 36. Work out the rest of the path of the knight and enter the relevant number in each empty cell of the grid. The knight moves either two squares horizontally followed by one square vertically, or two squares vertically followed by one square horizontally.

Word Square

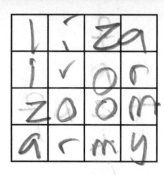

_____ Minnelli: US actress

_____ Novello: Welsh composer

Move rapidly

Military body

Place four four-letter words to solve each clue such that the words are spelled out both across and down in each of the four rows and columns.

Diamond 26

The sum of the six triangles that compose each hexagon is 26. Can you place numbers from 1–9 in each empty triangle to complete the puzzle? You cannot repeat a number within a hexagon.

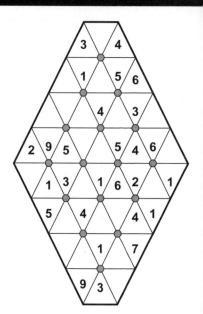

Word Definer

Can you choose the correct meaning of the following word from the options underneath?

OREAD

1 A bull that is over three years old

2 Yellow in color

3 A mountain nymph

Word Pyramid

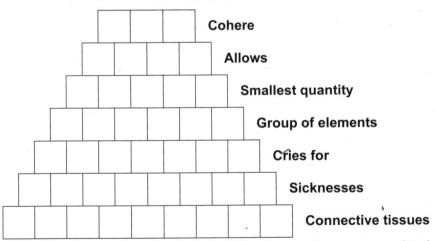

Cohere

Allows

Smallest quantity

Group of elements

Cries for

Sicknesses

Connective tissues

Fill each brick with a single letter to build a pyramid. Each row contains the same bricks as the row beneath but with one missing—however the order may vary. Each row must spell out a word that matches its clue.

Number Square

	-	9	+		0
+	■	x	■	-	
	÷	2	-		-5
-	■	÷	■	x	
	-		-		3
3		18		-9	

Enter the remaining numbers from 1–9 once in each of the empty squares to complete the sums correctly. Perform calculations from left to right and from top to bottom.

Number Tower

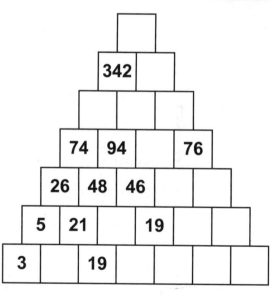

Fill the tower so that every square contains a number. The value of each square in the number tower is the sum of the two squares directly under it.

142

Bridges

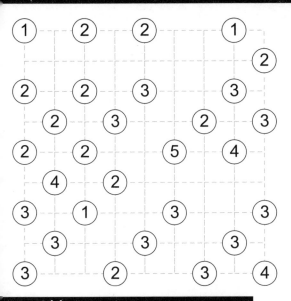

Connect all the circles (which represent islands) into a single interconnected group. The number in a circle represents the number of bridges that connect that island to other islands. Bridges can only be created horizontally or vertically, with no more than two bridges between any pair of islands. Bridges cannot cross any other bridges.

Killer 6x6

3		14	7		8
12				8	
	5	9	15		
					13
9		6		6	
11					

Place the numbers 1–6 exactly once per row, column, and 3 x 2 bold-lined box. Additionally the sum total of the squares in each dashed-line shape must match the total given in that shape, and you may not repeat a number within a dashed-line shape.

B	2	E		
				4
				C
E	1	A	3	
	D4			

Each square contains a letter and a number. Place 1–5 and A–E once in each row and column to fill the grid. Each combination from A1 through to E5 also appears exactly once in the puzzle.

King's Journey

4	5	7	8	12	13	14
3	6	9	11	18	17	15
2	1	10	24	23	19	16
40	41	47	46	25	22	20
39	42	48	49	45	26	21
37	38	43	44	32	30	27
36	35	34	33	31	29	28

Deduce the journey of a chess king as it visits each square of the grid exactly once, starting at 1 and ending at 49. The king may move one square at a time in any direction, including diagonally.

144

TEEM

deem

deer

poer

pooir

POUR

Can you climb the rungs of this word ladder? Change only one letter at each step in order to move from the bottom to the top, and do not rearrange the order of the letters.

Wordwheel

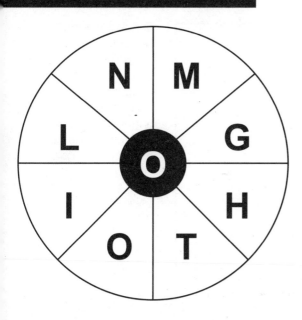

How many words of three or more letters can you find in this wordwheel? Form words by using the letter in the center of the wheel plus a selection from the outer wheel, where no letter may be used more than once in any word.

There is at least one nine-letter word to be found.

Jigsaw 6x6

Place the numbers 1–6 once in each row, column, and bold-lined jigsaw region composed of six cells.

		1			
			2		4
5		3			
1	3				

Find The Mines

Find all the mines in the grid. Numbers in certain squares indicate how many mines there are in the neighboring squares, including diagonally touching squares. Mines cannot be placed in squares with numbers.

	2			1	1		
			1	2	3	4	
2		2					3
	1			1	2		
		1	1				
2						1	
		2		2			0
	2					2	

146

ABC Logic

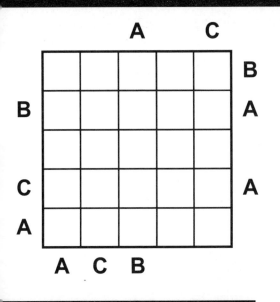

Place the letters A, B, and C exactly once in each row and column. Each row and column has two blank cells. The letters at the edge of a row/column indicate which of the letters is the first/last to appear in that row/column.

Battleships

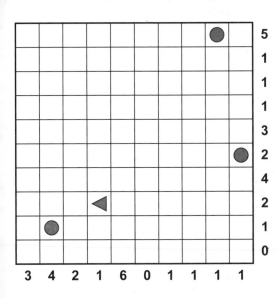

Locate the position of each of the ships listed below. Numbers around the edge tell you the number of ship segments in each row and column of the puzzle. Ships are surrounded on all sides by water, including diagonally.

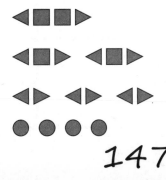

147

Kakuro

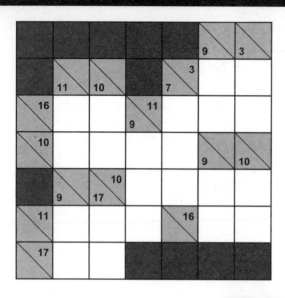

Fill the white squares so that the total in each across or down run of cells matches the total at the start of that run. You must use the numbers from 1–9 only and cannot repeat a number in a run.

Killer 6x6

6		10	10		8
13	8		7		
			9	11	
	10	10			
				7	7
5		5			

Place the numbers 1–6 exactly once per row, column, and 3 x 2 bold-lined box. Additionally the sum total of the squares in each dashed-line shape must match the total given in that shape, and you may not repeat a number within a dashed-line shape.

148

Hidden Words

Can you find the colors hidden in the sentences below?

1 Very hot curry was problematic as rice incident led to pilau burn.

2 After a late night, Oscar lethargically got up the next morning.

Pathfinder

I	T	E	B	T	I	M	A	R
N	U	E	A	E	N	T	I	F
I	R	T	U	A	E	E	T	L
N	A	I	X	R	G	C	W	O
O	L	T	I	B	O	I	G	A
Y	I	E	T	E	R	N	R	L
R	T	N	G	E	N	N	A	E
C	E	M	A	T	I	A	B	N
E	T	I	M	O	L	O	D	A

Moving from letter to adjacent letter, can you find a path that visits every square and spells out the names of several **mineral ores**? Start on the shaded square.

149

Wordwheel

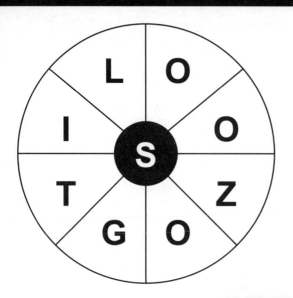

How many words of three or more letters can you find in this wordwheel? Form words by using the letter in the center of the wheel plus a selection from the outer wheel, where no letter may be used more than once in any word.

There is at least one nine-letter word to be found.

Word Square

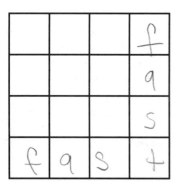

Roman poet

Permit to enter

Egyptian goddess

Run quickly

Place four four-letter words to solve each clue such that the words are spelled out both across and down in each of the four rows and columns.

150

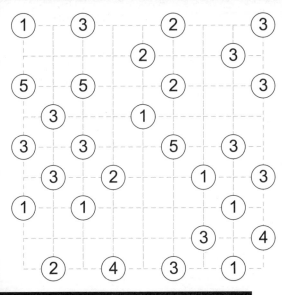

Connect all the circles (which represent islands) into a single interconnected group. The number in a circle represents the number of bridges that connect that island to other islands. Bridges can only be created horizontally or vertically, with no more than two bridges between any pair of islands. Bridges cannot cross any other bridges.

Calcudoku

7+	36x		30x		
	9+		11+	7+	24x
6x					
		12x			6+
8x		9+	9+		
10x				7+	

Place the numbers from 1–6 once in each row and column, obeying the sums in the bold-lined regions. Numbers may repeat within the bold-lined regions. With subtraction always take the lower numbers away from the highest number in a region, and with division divide the highest number by the lower numbers.

King's Journey

3	2	1	34		31	
4			36			29
5					46	
8				49	48	
					41	
	13		20	40	25	24
11		14	15			

Deduce the journey of a chess king as it visits each square of the grid exactly once, starting at 1 and ending at 49. The king may move one square at a time in any direction, including diagonally.

Futoshiki

Place the numbers 1–5 exactly once in each row and column. The greater than and less than signs (">" and "<" respectively) indicate where one cell is greater/less than the adjacent cell.

152

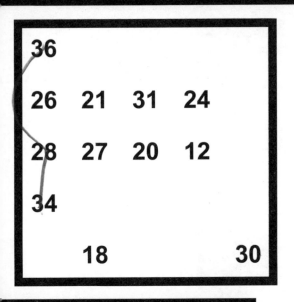

36			
26	21	31	24
28	27	20	12
34			
	18		30

Three of the numbers in this box add up to 98. But can you work out what those three numbers are?

ABCDoku

			3	
E			A	B
			1	A
	4			5
4		D		C

Each square contains a letter and a number. Place 1–5 and A–E once in each row and column to fill the grid. Each combination from A1 through to E5 also appears exactly once in the puzzle.

Kakuro

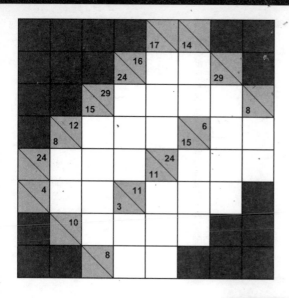

Fill the white squares so that the total in each across or down run of cells matches the total at the start of that run. You must use the numbers from 1–9 only and cannot repeat a number in a run.

Word Square

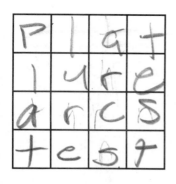

Flat region

Tempt

Curves

Check

Place four four-letter words to solve each clue such that the words are spelled out both across and down in each of the four rows and columns.

25	30	1	16	19	32
2	17	28	31	8	15
29	34	9	18	33	20
10	3	24	27	14	7
23	26	5	12	21	36
4	11	22	25	6	13

The grid represents the moves of a chess knight as it visits each square exactly once, starting at 1 and ending at 36. Work out the rest of the path of the knight and enter the relevant number in each empty cell of the grid. The knight moves either two squares horizontally followed by one square vertically, or two squares vertically followed by one square horizontally.

Find The Sum

		12	
15		25	49
23	44	27	35
18			
31		29	33

Three of the numbers in this box add up to 118. But can you work out what those three numbers are?

Word Square

		m	t
		e	i
m	e	a	n
t	i	n	y

Garment edges

Wicked

Abstract Spanish artist

Narrow opening

Place four four-letter words to solve each clue such that the words are spelled out both across and down in each of the four rows and columns.

Word Egg

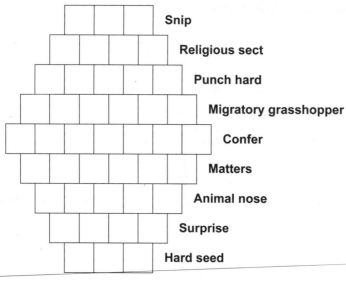

Snip

Religious sect

Punch hard

Migratory grasshopper

Confer

Matters

Animal nose

Surprise

Hard seed

Crack this word egg by answering the clue to the right of each row. Each answer is an anagram of the row above with either one extra or one less letter.

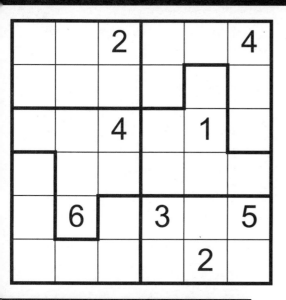

Place the numbers 1–6 once in each row, column, and bold-lined jigsaw region composed of six cells.

Wordwheel

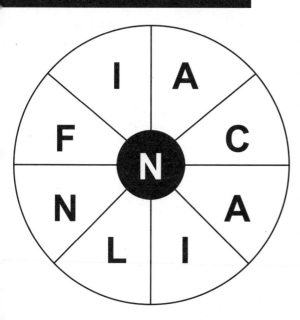

How many words of three or more letters can you find in this wordwheel? Form words by using the letter in the center of the wheel plus a selection from the outer wheel, where no letter may be used more than once in any word.

There is at least one nine-letter word to be found.

157

Fillomino

Fill every empty square with a number of any value. Each number must form part of a continuous region of squares of size specified by the number. Two different regions with the same number of squares cannot touch horizontally/vertically. Some regions may have no preprinted numbers at all, while others may have multiple preprinted numbers.

1			6		
		6		1	
	2		1	5	
	5	5		6	
	7		6		
		1			1

Futoshiki

Place the numbers 1–5 exactly once in each row and column. The greater than and less than signs (">" and "<" respectively) indicate where one cell is greater/less than the adjacent cell.

158

Number Square

1	x		x		24
x	■	-	■	x	
8	-	5	+	7	12
-	■	x	■	÷	
2	-		x		-15
6		-7		18	

Enter the remaining numbers from 1–9 once in each of the empty squares to complete the sums correctly. Perform calculations from left to right and from top to bottom.

Knight's Tour

			4	31	24
	3			16	5
	28	17	6	5	
2	7		35		9
	20		8	33	22
12	1	36		0	

The grid represents the moves of a chess knight as it visits each square exactly once, starting at 1 and ending at 36. Work out the rest of the path of the knight and enter the relevant number in each empty cell of the grid. The knight moves either two squares horizontally followed by one square vertically, or two squares vertically followed by one square horizontally.

159

Word Square

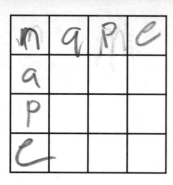

Back of the neck

Very keen

Yearn deeply

Paradise garden

Place four four-letter words to solve each clue such that the words are spelled out both across and down in each of the four rows and columns.

Find The Sum

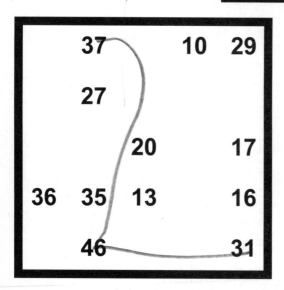

Three of the numbers in this box add up to 114. But can you work out what those three numbers are?

Can you choose the correct meaning of the following word from the options underneath?

MALAR

1 A minor sickness

2 Of the cheek

3 An aggressive person

Word Pyramid

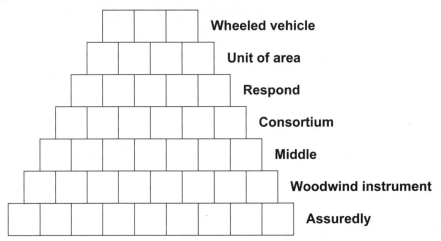

Wheeled vehicle

Unit of area

Respond

Consortium

Middle

Woodwind instrument

Assuredly

Fill each brick with a single letter to build a pyramid. Each row contains the same bricks as the row beneath but with one missing—however the order may vary. Each row must spell out a word that matches its clue.

Number Square

6	x	8	x	2	96
x	■	+	■	x	
9	-	4	x	5	25
x	■	+	■	+	
7	-	3	x	1	4
378		15		11	

Enter the remaining numbers from 1–9 once in each of the empty squares to complete the sums correctly. Perform calculations from left to right and from top to bottom.

3^2
54
17
378

Dominoes

0	0	1	1	5	6	0	0
2	3	3	1	2	4	6	2
6	2	1	3	0	4	0	3
5	6	4	2	3	3	2	5
5	1	4	1	3	0	4	0
5	3	2	4	6	5	6	5
4	6	2	1	4	5	6	1

Place a full set of regular dominoes into this grid, where 0 represents a blank. Use the chart alongside to tick off the dominoes you've already placed. Each domino is used once only.

0	1	2	3	4	5	6	
							0
							1
							2
							3
							4
							5
							6

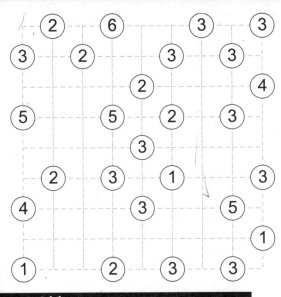

Connect all the circles (which represent islands) into a single interconnected group. The number in a circle represents the number of bridges that connect that island to other islands. Bridges can only be created horizontally or vertically, with no more than two bridges between any pair of islands. Bridges cannot cross any other bridges.

Killer 6x6

7		6	11		
10			5		12
8	11		10		
				11	
	12		6	12	
5					

Place the numbers 1–6 exactly once per row, column, and 3 x 2 bold-lined box. Additionally the sum total of the squares in each dashed-line shape must match the total given in that shape, and you may not repeat a number within a dashed-line shape.

163

ABCDoku

		5	E	
B1		E	2	
E		D	C	
5				E3

Each square contains a letter and a number. Place 1–5 and A–E once in each row and column to fill the grid. Each combination from A1 through to E5 also appears exactly once in the puzzle.

King's Journey

1		4			7	
					11	
31		47	45	35	13	
	49		44		36	
				40		
25	27	28	39	38		
			21		18	

Deduce the journey of a chess king as it visits each square of the grid exactly once, starting at 1 and ending at 49. The king may move one square at a time in any direction, including diagonally.

Word Square

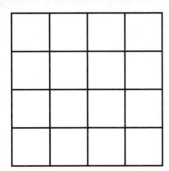

Large wading bird

Dwell

Hero

Exchange for money

Place four four-letter words to solve each clue such that the words are spelled out both across and down in each of the four rows and columns.

Wordwheel

How many words of three or more letters can you find in this wordwheel? Form words by using the letter in the center of the wheel plus a selection from the outer wheel, where no letter may be used more than once in any word.

There is at least one nine-letter word to be found.

Jigsaw 6x6

Place the numbers 1–6 once in each row, column, and bold-lined jigsaw region composed of six cells.

	3				
			1		
	2		6		
3					2
				4	

Calcudoku

Place the numbers from 1–6 once in each row and column, obeying the sums in the bold-lined regions. Numbers may repeat within the bold-lined regions. With subtraction always take the lower numbers away from the highest number in a region, and with division divide the highest number by the lower numbers.

11+	6+	11+	30x	9+	
					4x
	8x		1-		
		2-	1-	30x	
11+				7+	
13+				10x	

ABC Logic

Place the letters A, B, and C exactly once in each row and column. Each row and column has two blank cells. The letters at the edge of a row/column indicate which of the letters is the first/last to appear in that row/column.

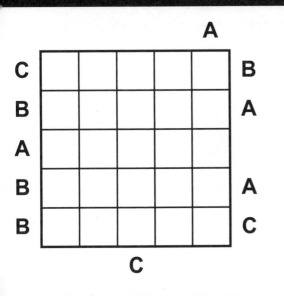

Fillomino

Fill every empty square with a number of any value. Each number must form part of a continuous region of squares of size specified by the number. Two different regions with the same number of squares cannot touch horizontally/vertically. Some regions may have no preprinted numbers at all, while others may have multiple preprinted numbers.

	2		4		1
	5	5			
	5	1			
			3	5	
			6	4	
2		2		1	

Kakuro

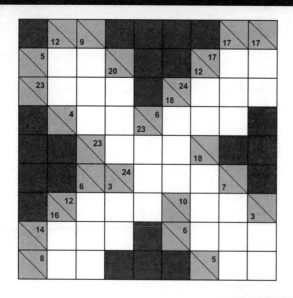

Fill the white squares so that the total in each across or down run of cells matches the total at the start of that run. You must use the numbers from 1–9 only and cannot repeat a number in a run.

Dominoes

4	1	4	4	0	0	3	2
6	0	2	2	4	2	3	6
0	1	5	6	6	3	3	3
0	6	3	1	5	6	1	4
5	1	1	4	2	4	2	3
5	3	4	0	5	2	6	5
1	1	5	0	6	0	2	5

Place a full set of regular dominoes into this grid, where 0 represents a blank. Use the chart alongside to tick off the dominoes you've already placed. Each domino is used once only.

0	1	2	3	4	5	6	
							0
							1
							2
							3
							4
							5
							6

Can you find the words associated with Halloween hidden in the sentences below?

1 Goalkeeper praised for clean sheet, though ostensibly he was never tested.

2 Medical trial participants to undergo blind testing of new medicine.

King's Journey

36	35			29	1	2
			33	30	28	3
49	47	45	40		27	4
		44		26	23	5
17			25	24	22	6
16	18	19	20	21	10	7
15	14	13	12	11	9	8

Deduce the journey of a chess king as it visits each square of the grid exactly once, starting at 1 and ending at 49. The king may move one square at a time in any direction, including diagonally.

169

Wordwheel

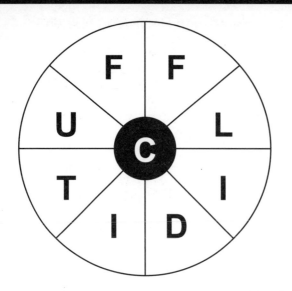

How many words of three or more letters can you find in this wordwheel? Form words by using the letter in the center of the wheel plus a selection from the outer wheel, where no letter may be used more than once in any word.

There is at least one nine-letter word to be found.

Word Square

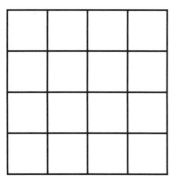

Golf stroke

US state

Recording medium

At that time

Place four four-letter words to solve each clue such that the words are spelled out both across and down in each of the four rows and columns.

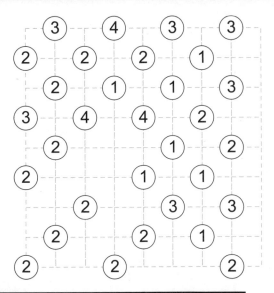

Connect all the circles (which represent islands) into a single interconnected group. The number in a circle represents the number of bridges that connect that island to other islands. Bridges can only be created horizontally or vertically, with no more than two bridges between any pair of islands. Bridges cannot cross any other bridges.

Calcudoku

2-	15+			2x	
	1-		3÷	10+	
2÷	2÷			15+	
	2-		15x		
5-			10+		6x
24x		7+			

Place the numbers from 1–6 once in each row and column, obeying the sums in the bold-lined regions. Numbers may repeat within the bold-lined regions. With subtraction always take the lower numbers away from the highest number in a region, and with division divide the highest number by the lower numbers.

King's Journey

	7	4		45		
9					49	48
11		1				
		16	35	38	40	41
14		25	34	36		
	20		23			29

Deduce the journey of a chess king as it visits each square of the grid exactly once, starting at 1 and ending at 49. The king may move one square at a time in any direction, including diagonally.

Futoshiki

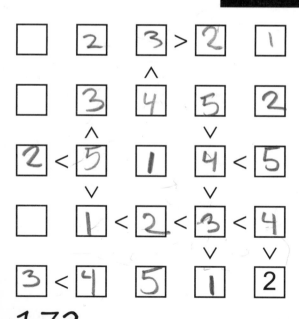

Place the numbers 1–5 exactly once in each row and column. The greater than and less than signs (">" and "<" respectively) indicate where one cell is greater/less than the adjacent cell.

172

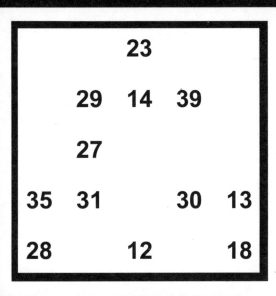

Three of the numbers in this box add up to 102. But can you work out what those three numbers are?

ABC Logic

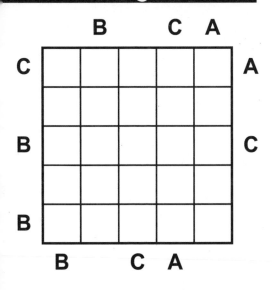

Place the letters A, B, and C exactly once in each row and column. Each row and column has two blank cells. The letters at the edge of a row/column indicate which of the letters is the first/last to appear in that row/column.

Bridges

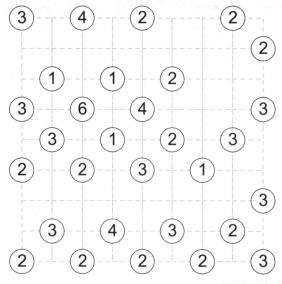

Connect all the circles (which represent islands) into a single interconnected group. The number in a circle represents the number of bridges that connect that island to other islands. Bridges can only be created horizontally or vertically, with no more than two bridges between any pair of islands. Bridges cannot cross any other bridges.

Word Square

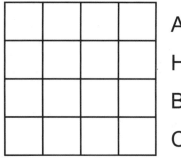

Ascend

Hotels

Break

Catch sight of

Place four four-letter words to solve each clue such that the words are spelled out both across and down in each of the four rows and columns.

174

			13		27
			28		
	1		15		5
			24		
8			35	6	
19	10		32	21	36

The grid represents the moves of a chess knight as it visits each square exactly once, starting at 1 and ending at 36. Work out the rest of the path of the knight and enter the relevant number in each empty cell of the grid. The knight moves either two squares horizontally followed by one square vertically, or two squares vertically followed by one square horizontally.

Find The Sum

	28	17		
21	12		13	20
37	10			
33	34			
			18	19

Three of the numbers in this box add up to 99. But can you work out what those three numbers are?

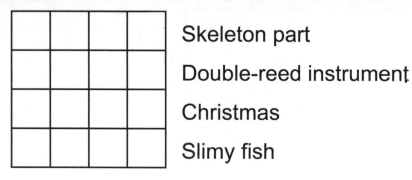

Word Square

Skeleton part

Double-reed instrument

Christmas

Slimy fish

Place four four-letter words to solve each clue such that the words are spelled out both across and down in each of the four rows and columns.

Word Egg

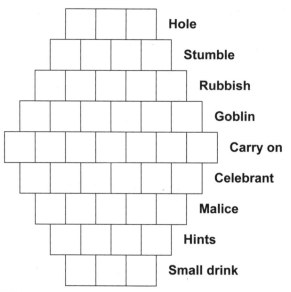

Hole

Stumble

Rubbish

Goblin

Carry on

Celebrant

Malice

Hints

Small drink

Crack this word egg by answering the clue to the right of each row. Each answer is an anagram of the row above with either one extra or one less letter.

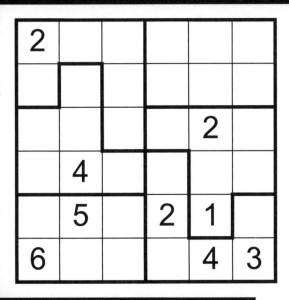

Place the numbers 1–6 once in each row, column, and bold-lined jigsaw region composed of six cells.

Wordwheel

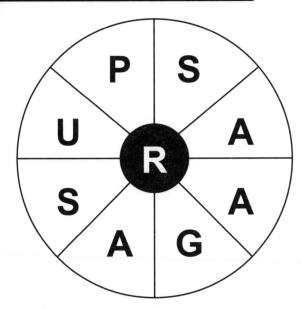

How many words of three or more letters can you find in this wordwheel? Form words by using the letter in the center of the wheel plus a selection from the outer wheel, where no letter may be used more than once in any word.

There is at least one nine-letter word to be found.

Fillomino

Fill every empty square with a number of any value. Each number must form part of a continuous region of squares of size specified by the number. Two different regions with the same number of squares cannot touch horizontally/vertically. Some regions may have no preprinted numbers at all, while others may have multiple preprinted numbers.

					4
	3			1	
	5	1	3	3	
	5	6	6	7	
	3			6	
1					

Futoshiki

Place the numbers 1–5 exactly once in each row and column. The greater than and less than signs (">" and "<" respectively) indicate where one cell is greater/less than the adjacent cell.

□   □ < □   □ > □
              V
[4] □   □ < □   □
V   V
□ > □   □   □   □
                        V
□   □   □ > □ < □
        V   ^
□ < □ > □   □   □

178

Enter the remaining numbers from 1–9 once in each of the empty squares to complete the sums correctly. Perform calculations from left to right and from top to bottom.

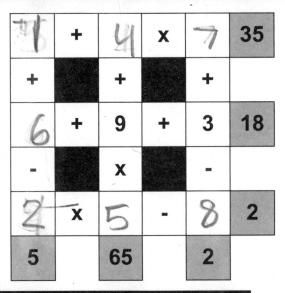

7	+	4	x	7	35
+		+		+	
6	+	9	+	3	18
-		x		-	
2	x	5	-	8	2
5		65		2	

$$13\overline{)65}$$

Knight's Tour

12		6	29	14	25
7		13	24	3	30
	11	34			17
	8	18			4
10	21	2			19
1	36	9	20	3	

The grid represents the moves of a chess knight as it visits each square exactly once, starting at 1 and ending at 36. Work out the rest of the path of the knight and enter the relevant number in each empty cell of the grid. The knight moves either two squares horizontally followed by one square vertically, or two squares vertically followed by one square horizontally.

Word Square

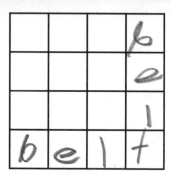

Tins

Vocal solo

Pen points

Band worn about the waist

Place four four-letter words to solve each clue such that the words are spelled out both across and down in each of the four rows and columns.

Find The Sum

42			17	20
23				34
	19		21	
			37	25
39			35	18

Three of the numbers in this box add up to 115. But can you work out what those three numbers are?

Word Definer

Can you choose the correct meaning of the following word from the options underneath?

TRITIUM

1 A flower with three petals

2 A fire-breathing dragon

3 An isotope of hydrogen

Word Pyramid

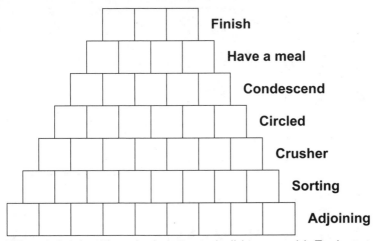

	Finish
	Have a meal
	Condescend
	Circled
	Crusher
	Sorting
	Adjoining

Fill each brick with a single letter to build a pyramid. Each row contains the same bricks as the row beneath but with one missing—however the order may vary. Each row must spell out a word that matches its clue.

Number Square

Enter the remaining numbers from 1–9 once in each of the empty squares to complete the sums correctly. Perform calculations from left to right and from top to bottom.

The number square grid:

7	x	3	x	2	42
-	■	-	■	x	
5	-	4	-	6	-5
x	■	+	■	+	
8	+	1	÷	9	1
16		0		21	

Dominoes

2	2	4	0	1	4	4	3
0	6	2	1	0	5	6	3
2	6	4	3	3	5	6	3
1	1	4	6	1	5	0	1
4	4	2	1	3	0	5	2
0	1	6	2	6	5	6	5
0	5	3	4	5	3	2	0

Place a full set of regular dominoes into this grid, where 0 represents a blank. Use the chart alongside to tick off the dominoes you've already placed. Each domino is used once only.

0	1	2	3	4	5	6	
							0
							1
							2
							3
							4
							5
							6

182

Bridges

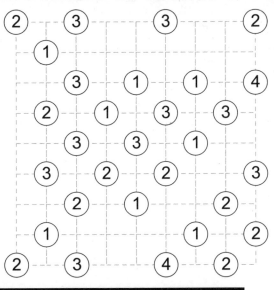

Connect all the circles (which represent islands) into a single interconnected group. The number in a circle represents the number of bridges that connect that island to other islands. Bridges can only be created horizontally or vertically, with no more than two bridges between any pair of islands. Bridges cannot cross any other bridges.

Fillomino

Fill every empty square with a number of any value. Each number must form part of a continuous region of squares of size specified by the number. Two different regions with the same number of squares cannot touch horizontally/vertically. Some regions may have no preprinted numbers at all, while others may have multiple preprinted numbers.

			4	7		
2					7	1
			2		3	
		4		3		
4	4					3
			7	7		

ABC Logic

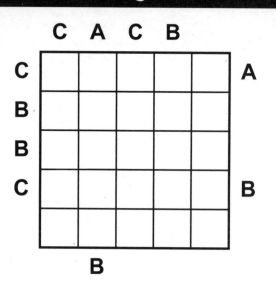

Place the letters A, B, and C exactly once in each row and column. Each row and column has two blank cells. The letters at the edge of a row/column indicate which of the letters is the first/last to appear in that row/column.

King's Journey

33	32				27	
	35	37	38	39		
11		49	46			
		47				23
1	9		43			
	5				20	
	4		15			17

Deduce the journey of a chess king as it visits each square of the grid exactly once, starting at 1 and ending at 49. The king may move one square at a time in any direction, including diagonally.

184

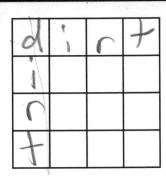

Solid ground

Febrile condition

Deprived of sensation

Liability

Place four four-letter words to solve each clue such that the words are spelled out both across and down in each of the four rows and columns.

Wordwheel

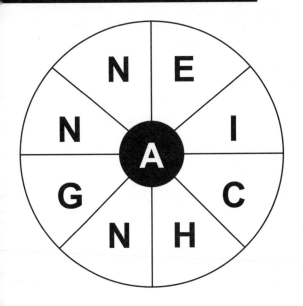

How many words of three or more letters can you find in this wordwheel? Form words by using the letter in the center of the wheel plus a selection from the outer wheel, where no letter may be used more than once in any word.

There is at least one nine-letter word to be found.

Jigsaw 6x6

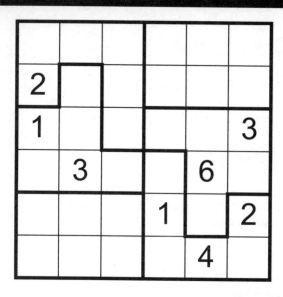

Place the numbers 1–6 once in each row, column, and bold-lined jigsaw region composed of six cells.

Calcudoku

30x	1-		8+		
	150x		12x		10+
12x	1-	4-	1-		8+
			13+		
		2-			

Place the numbers from 1–6 once in each row and column, obeying the sums in the bold-lined regions. Numbers may repeat within the bold-lined regions. With subtraction always take the lower numbers away from the highest number in a region, and with division divide the highest number by the lower numbers.

Fill every empty square with a number of any value. Each number must form part of a continuous region of squares of size specified by the number. Two different regions with the same number of squares cannot touch horizontally/vertically. Some regions may have no preprinted numbers at all, while others may have multiple preprinted numbers.

			6		1
1			3		5
		1		5	
	5		3		
5		4			2
2		5			

Word Pyramid

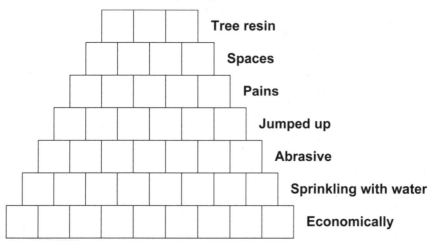

Tree resin

Spaces

Pains

Jumped up

Abrasive

Sprinkling with water

Economically

Fill each brick with a single letter to build a pyramid. Each row contains the same bricks as the row beneath but with one missing—however the order may vary. Each row must spell out a word that matches its clue.

Word Egg

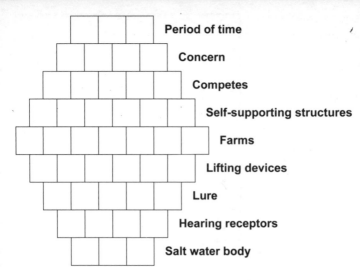

Clue
Period of time
Concern
Competes
Self-supporting structures
Farms
Lifting devices
Lure
Hearing receptors
Salt water body

Crack this word egg by answering the clue to the right of each row. Each answer is an anagram of the row above with either one extra or one less letter.

Dominoes

0	5	6	1	3	3	4	4
6	2	4	4	2	5	4	4
6	6	2	5	2	0	1	1
2	6	1	0	6	0	5	5
0	6	1	5	0	3	0	1
3	4	5	1	2	2	4	3
3	1	3	5	3	2	0	6

Place a full set of regular dominoes into this grid, where 0 represents a blank. Use the chart alongside to tick off the dominoes you've already placed. Each domino is used once only.

0	1	2	3	4	5	6	
							0
							1
							2
							3
							4
							5
							6

Can you find the flowers hidden in the sentences below?

1 Gravity was famously discovered by Sir Isaac Newton.

2 Other cleaning companies sweep up as dustpan syndicate goes bust.

King's Journey

15	16	18	19	30	31	32
14	17	20	29	46	34	33
13	21	28	45	49	47	35
12	22	27	44	48	41	36
11	23	26	43	42	40	37
9	10	24	25	39	38	1
8	7	6	5	4	3	2

Deduce the journey of a chess king as it visits each square of the grid exactly once, starting at 1 and ending at 49. The king may move one square at a time in any direction, including diagonally.

189

Wordwheel

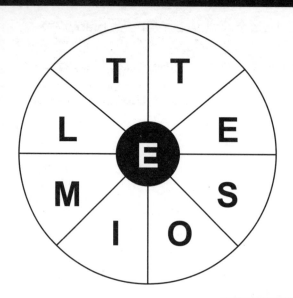

How many words of three or more letters can you find in this wordwheel? Form words by using the letter in the center of the wheel plus a selection from the outer wheel, where no letter may be used more than once in any word.

There is at least one nine-letter word to be found.

Fillomino

Fill every empty square with a number of any value. Each number must form part of a continuous region of squares of size specified by the number. Two different regions with the same number of squares cannot touch horizontally/vertically. Some regions may have no preprinted numbers at all, while others may have multiple preprinted numbers.

3					7
	3		6	7	7
1					
					6
1	6	1		3	
2					6

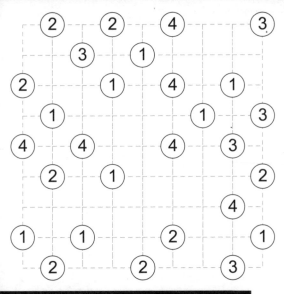

Connect all the circles (which represent islands) into a single interconnected group. The number in a circle represents the number of bridges that connect that island to other islands. Bridges can only be created horizontally or vertically, with no more than two bridges between any pair of islands. Bridges cannot cross any other bridges.

Calcudoku

72x	6+			9+	14+
		3+			
10+			12x		
10+			11+		
6÷	12x	14+			2x
		11+			

Place the numbers from 1–6 once in each row and column, obeying the sums in the bold-lined regions. Numbers may repeat within the bold-lined regions. With subtraction always take the lower numbers away from the highest number in a region, and with division divide the highest number by the lower numbers.

King's Journey

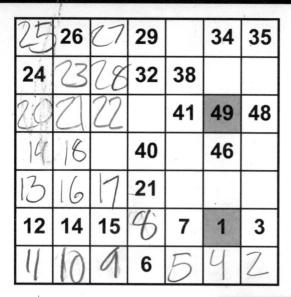

25	26	27	29		34	35
24	23	28	32	38		
20	21	22		41	49	48
19	18		40		46	
13	16	17	21			
12	14	15	9	7	1	3
11	10	9	6	5	4	2

Deduce the journey of a chess king as it visits each square of the grid exactly once, starting at 1 and ending at 49. The king may move one square at a time in any direction, including diagonally.

Futoshiki

☐ > ☐   ☐ < ☐   [2]
        ∨   ∧
☐   ☐   ☐   ☐   ☐
    ∧   ∧
☐   ☐   ☐   ☐   ☐
                    ∧
☐ > ☐ > ☐ > ☐   ☐
    ∨
☐ > ☐   ☐ > ☐   ☐

Place the numbers 1–5 exactly once in each row and column. The greater than and less than signs (">" and "<" respectively) indicate where one cell is greater/less than the adjacent cell.

192

Find The Sum

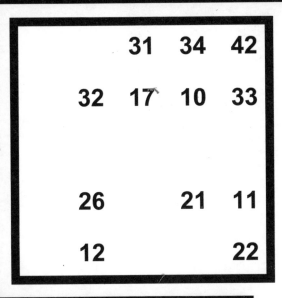

	31	34	42
32	17	10	33
26		21	11
12			22

Three of the numbers in this box add up to 47. But can you work out what those three numbers are?

ABC Logic

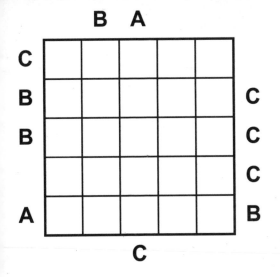

Place the letters A, B, and C exactly once in each row and column. Each row and column has two blank cells. The letters at the edge of a row/column indicate which of the letters is the first/last to appear in that row/column.

193

Bridges

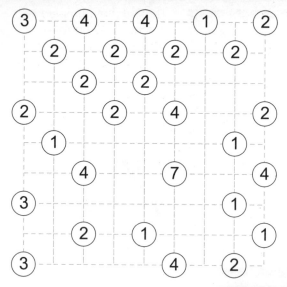

Connect all the circles (which represent islands) into a single interconnected group. The number in a circle represents the number of bridges that connect that island to other islands. Bridges can only be created horizontally or vertically, with no more than two bridges between any pair of islands. Bridges cannot cross any other bridges.

Word Pyramid

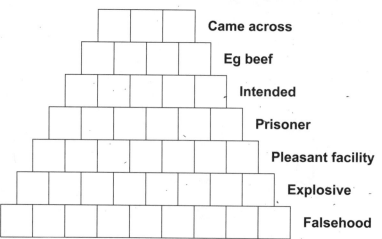

Came across

Eg beef

Intended

Prisoner

Pleasant facility

Explosive

Falsehood

Fill each brick with a single letter to build a pyramid. Each row contains the same bricks as the row beneath but with one missing—however the order may vary. Each row must spell out a word that matches its clue.

194

Symbol Values

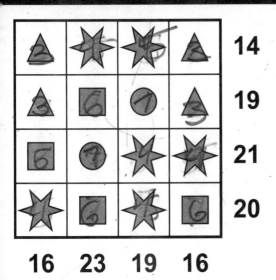

14
19
21
20

16   23   19   16

Each of the four shapes represents a positive whole number. The sum of the shapes in each row and column is displayed at the end of each row and column. Using this information can you work out the numerical value of each shape?

Wordwheel

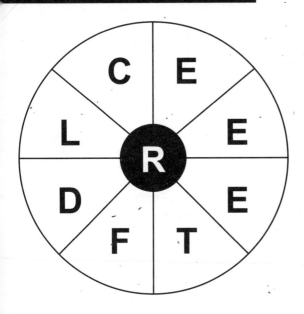

How many words of three or more letters can you find in this wordwheel? Form words by using the letter in the center of the wheel plus a selection from the outer wheel, where no letter may be used more than once in any word.

There is at least one nine-letter word to be found.

ABC Logic

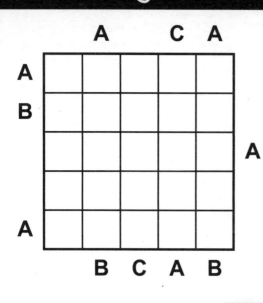

Place the letters A, B, and C exactly once in each row and column. Each row and column has two blank cells. The letters at the edge of a row/column indicate which of the letters is the first/last to appear in that row/column.

Calcudoku

3-		2-			12x
10+	2÷	8+	9+	9+	
4-		9+			11+
7+	1-	12x	4÷		
		2-			

Place the numbers from 1–6 once in each row and column, obeying the sums in the bold-lined regions. Numbers may repeat within the bold-lined regions. With subtraction always take the lower numbers away from the highest number in a region, and with division divide the highest number by the lower numbers.

Fillomino

Fill every empty square with a number of any value. Each number must form part of a continuous region of squares of size specified by the number. Two different regions with the same number of squares cannot touch horizontally/vertically. Some regions may have no preprinted numbers at all, while others may have multiple preprinted numbers.

	2				
4	1	7		2	
	5			2	
	4			1	
	2		1	4	1
				4	

Word Pyramid

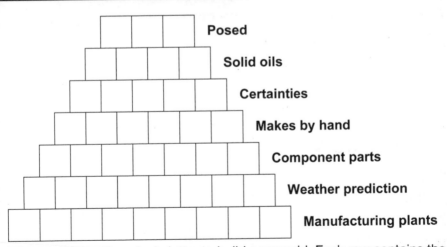

Posed

Solid oils

Certainties

Makes by hand

Component parts

Weather prediction

Manufacturing plants

Fill each brick with a single letter to build a pyramid. Each row contains the same bricks as the row beneath but with one missing—however the order may vary. Each row must spell out a word that matches its clue.

197

Word Egg

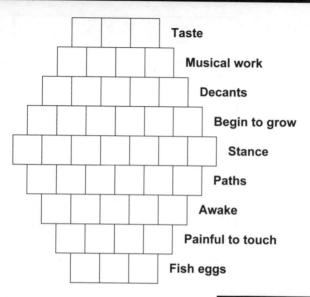

Taste

Musical work

Decants

Begin to grow

Stance

Paths

Awake

Painful to touch

Fish eggs

Crack this word egg by answering the clue to the right of each row. Each answer is an anagram of the row above with either one extra or one less letter.

Find The Sum

Three of the numbers in this box add up to 65. But can you work out what those three numbers are?

				35
22				
33	38	42	37	34
30			15	28
	19		39	

198

Hidden Words

Can you find the emotions hidden in the sentences below?

1 No-one knows what redundancy is like until they are made unemployed.

2 Elite university provides Ireland's best students with superb education.

King's Journey

	34		39		49	
32		37			48	
				43	45	11
23	25			28		
19			27		9	
				1	7	6
		15			4	

Deduce the journey of a chess king as it visits each square of the grid exactly once, starting at 1 and ending at 49. The king may move one square at a time in any direction, including diagonally.

Fillomino

Fill every empty square with a number of any value. Each number must form part of a continuous region of squares of size specified by the number. Two different regions with the same number of squares cannot touch horizontally/vertically. Some regions may have no preprinted numbers at all, while others may have multiple preprinted numbers.

	7	1		
				2
	1	3	3	1
	9	9	1	6
1				
			9	6

Futoshiki

Place the numbers 1–5 exactly once in each row and column. The greater than and less than signs (">" and "<" respectively) indicate where one cell is greater/less than the adjacent cell.

200

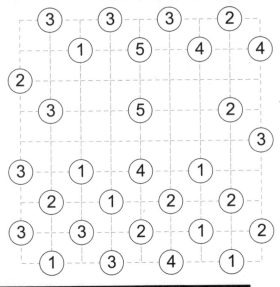

Connect all the circles (which represent islands) into a single interconnected group. The number in a circle represents the number of bridges that connect that island to other islands. Bridges can only be created horizontally or vertically, with no more than two bridges between any pair of islands. Bridges cannot cross any other bridges.

Knight's Tour

7	22	9	34	5	24
10	33	6	23	16	31
21	8	35	32	25	4
36	11	26	17	30	15
1	20	13	28	3	18
12	27	2	19	14	29

The grid represents the moves of a chess knight as it visits each square exactly once, starting at 1 and ending at 36. Work out the rest of the path of the knight and enter the relevant number in each empty cell of the grid. The knight moves either two squares horizontally followed by one square vertically, or two squares vertically followed by one square horizontally.

ABC Logic

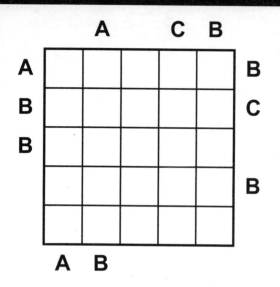

Place the letters A, B, and C exactly once in each row and column. Each row and column has two blank cells. The letters at the edge of a row/column indicate which of the letters is the first/last to appear in that row/column.

Word Pyramid

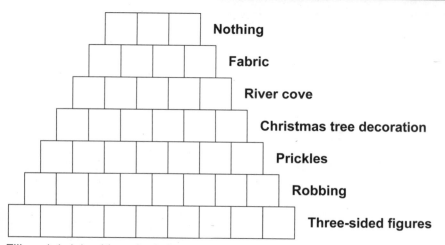

Nothing

Fabric

River cove

Christmas tree decoration

Prickles

Robbing

Three-sided figures

Fill each brick with a single letter to build a pyramid. Each row contains the same bricks as the row beneath but with one missing—however the order may vary. Each row must spell out a word that matches its clue.

202

Word Definer

Can you choose the correct meaning of the following word from the options underneath?

WACKE

1 A type of sandstone

2 Crazy

3 A dye extracted from soapwort

Binary Puzzle

0		1	1				0
	1		0			0	
				1			
	0			1	0		
1							
1	1		1		0		

Fill the grid with 0s and 1s such that 0 and 1 each occur four times in each row and column. The same digit cannot occur in more than two consecutive cells either horizontally or vertically. No whole row can repeat the same series of 0s and 1s as any other row, and no whole column can repeat the same series of 0s and 1s as any other column.

Number Square

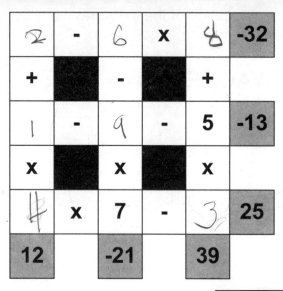

2	-	6	x	8	-32
+		-		+	
1	-	9	-	5	-13
x		x		x	
4	x	7	-	3	25
12		-21		39	

Enter the remaining numbers from 1–9 once in each of the empty squares to complete the sums correctly. Perform calculations from left to right and from top to bottom.

Find The Mines

	2	1			2		
	3			5			0
	3						
	2	2	2		2	2	
							2
			1				2
1		1		0	2		
	1				2		

Find all the mines in the grid. Numbers in certain squares indicate how many mines there are in the neighboring squares, including diagonally touching squares. Mines cannot be placed in squares with numbers.

204

Page 3

6	6	6	6	6	2
6	7	7	1	4	2
7	7	7	4	4	4
6	6	7	7	3	3
6	6	6	5	5	3
6	2	2	5	5	5

●	●	2	●		●		0
2						1	1
1			1	●	2		
●				1		●	3	●
	1	1				1	4	●
1				●	1		2	●
●	2	2		2		4	
			●	1		●	●	●

Page 4

A1	E4	C2	D3	B5
C4	D5	E3	B1	A2
B3	C1	A5	E2	D4
E5	B2	D1	A4	C3
D2	A3	B4	C5	E1

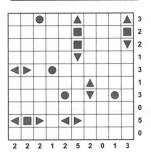

Page 5

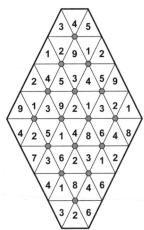

Snakeword:
Protected

Page 6

S	A	I	D
A	L	T	O
I	T	E	M
D	O	M	E

Solutions

Page 7

3	5	2	2	1	1	1	2
2	1	2	4	6	6	3	6
3	1	5	1	6	4	5	5
4	5	5	6	6	0	1	6
5	3	0	0	0	4	0	0
2	2	4	4	3	4	6	1
3	0	3	2	3	4	5	0

2 > 1 < 4 > 3   5
5   3   1   2 < 4
4   2   5   1   3
3   5   2 < 4   1
1   4 > 3   5 > 2

Page 8

4	23	10	29	2	25
11	28	3	24	17	30
22	5	34	9	26	1
35	12	27	18	31	16
6	21	14	33	8	19
13	36	7	20	15	32

G	F	I	G	E	R	S	S	P
N	T	S	N	C	E	W	O	E
I	R	G	A	N	A	M	L	E
R	O	O	D	C	E	O	F	C
S	W	M	T	S	C	R	S	H
V	O	I	I	R	A	O	N	E
S	S	N	F	E	K	I	D	S
K	I	V	I	T	A	T	R	E
G	N	I	D	D	E	W	S	S

Page 9

	3			7			
			2				3
	8						
	9	6			18	3	3
2	2	8					3
	2					3	
2				10			
2	2	2					

1	3	6	2	5	4
2	5	4	6	3	1
3	2	5	1	4	6
4	6	1	5	2	3
5	1	3	4	6	2
6	4	2	3	1	5

Page 10

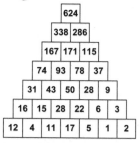

		624				
	338	286				
	167	171	115			
	74	93	78	37		
	31	43	50	28	9	
	16	15	28	22	6	3
12	4	11	17	5	1	2

BEST
WEST
WENT
WANT
WAND
HAND

Solutions

Page 11
Symbol Values:
Circle = 10
Square = 9
Triangle = 8
Star = 6

	A	N	T					
	G	N	A	T				
	G	R	A	N	T			
R	A	T	I	N	G			
G	R	A	N	I	T	E		
R	E	T	A	I	N			
	I	N	E	R	T			
	R	E	I	N				
	I	R	E					

Page 12
Word Definer:
1) A cotton fabric

Wordwheel:
Annoyance

Page 13
Word Scramble:
1 REPEATING
2 ABANDONED
3 INTERPRET

Find the Sum:
14, 15, 29

Page 14

		C		C	B	
A	A	C	B			
	B	A		C		C
C	C			A	B	B
B		B	C		A	
				A	B	C
		B		B	C	

0	1	0	0	1	1	0	1
0	1	1	0	0	1	1	0
1	0	0	1	0	0	1	1
1	0	1	0	1	1	0	0
0	1	0	1	1	0	0	1
0	0	1	1	0	1	1	0
1	1	0	0	1	0	0	1
1	0	1	1	0	0	1	0

Page 15

4	5	1	2	3	6
3	4	2	5	6	1
6	2	5	1	4	3
2	1	6	3	5	4
1	3	4	6	2	5
5	6	3	4	1	2

1	6	2	3	5	4
4	5	6	2	3	1
6	1	5	4	2	3
2	4	3	5	1	6
3	2	1	6	4	5
5	3	4	1	6	2

Solutions

Page 16

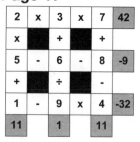

48	49	11	10	8	6	5
46	47	43	12	9	7	4
45	44	42	39	13	1	3
30	41	40	38	35	14	2
29	31	37	36	34	21	15
27	28	32	33	22	20	16
26	25	24	23	19	18	17

0	6	1	4	0	6	2	4
0	5	5	2	4	5	0	1
1	2	3	1	3	1	5	5
3	6	3	1	6	0	6	4
3	2	1	2	6	5	2	5
1	0	3	3	2	2	5	0
0	4	6	3	4	4	6	4

Page 17

2	x	3	x	7	42
x		+		+	
5	-	6	-	8	-9
+		÷		-	
1	-	9	x	4	-32
11		1		11	

Symbol Values:
Circle = 6
Square = 2
Triangle = 10
Star = 7

Page 18

Scales:
1 5
2 40
3 10

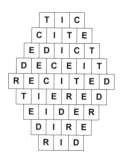

Page 19

Wordwheel:
Botanical

Solutions

Page 20

2	23	10	29	8	25
11	28	1	24	17	30
22	3	34	9	26	7
35	12	27	18	31	16
4	21	14	33	6	19
13	36	5	20	15	32

Word Scramble:
1 YESTERDAY
2 PRACTICAL
3 CONSISTED

Page 21

D3	B1	A2	E4	C5
E2	D4	C1	A5	B3
A1	E5	B4	C3	D2
B5	C2	E3	D1	A4
C4	A3	D5	B2	E1

1	0	1	0	1	0	1	0
1	1	0	1	0	1	0	0
0	0	1	1	0	0	1	1
1	1	0	0	1	1	0	0
0	1	0	0	1	0	1	1
0	0	1	1	0	1	1	0
1	0	0	1	0	1	0	1
0	1	1	0	1	0	0	1

Page 22

2	5	6	3	4	1
3	4	1	2	6	5
4	1	2	5	3	6
5	6	3	1	2	4
6	3	5	4	1	2
1	2	4	6	5	3

Page 23

MISS
MIST
MOST
MOAT
GOAT
GOAL

Solutions

Page 24
Find the Sum:
27, 33, 36

1		●	1		●		1
	●	2	1	1	2		●
1					1	●	2
2					1	2	
●	●		1		1		●
3				●		1	
2	●		3	●	3		
	●	3	●	3	●		0

Page 25
Hidden Words:
1 Rioja
2 Riesling

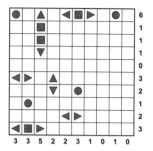

Page 26

8	x	2	x	4	64
+		+		-	
7	÷	1	+	6	13
x		x		+	
3	x	5	+	9	24
45		15		7	

2	6	3	4	5	1
5	3	1	6	4	2
6	1	5	2	3	4
1	4	6	5	2	3
3	2	4	1	6	5
4	5	2	3	1	6

Page 27

0	0	1	1	0	0	1	1
1	0	1	1	0	0	1	0
0	1	0	0	1	1	0	1
1	0	1	0	1	0	0	1
0	1	0	1	0	1	1	0
1	0	1	1	0	1	0	0
0	1	0	0	1	0	1	1
1	1	0	0	1	1	0	0

Symbol Values:
Circle = 3
Square = 8
Triangle = 1
Star = 2

Page 28
Snakeword:
Centenary

	3			4		5
	8				3	
18						
		9		2	10	
			3	3		
			3			
		2				
		2	2	3		5
					3	
	3		3		6	

Page 29

6	1	3	5	2	4
4	6	5	2	3	1
2	5	1	3	4	6
5	3	4	1	6	2
1	4	2	6	5	3
3	2	6	4	1	5

Wordwheel:
Commodity

Page 30

6	6	6	5	3	3
6	6	5	5	5	3
3	6	1	5	1	2
3	1	6	1	7	2
3	6	6	7	7	7
6	6	6	7	7	7

1 < 4   5   3 > 2
2^   5^   1   4^   3^
5^   1   3 > 2v < 4
4   3   2   1   5
3v > 2v < 4   5   1

Page 31
Word Scramble:
   1 TOLERANCE
   2 GUARANTEE
   3 GENERALLY

25	30	7	16	19	32
8	17	26	31	6	15
29	24	9	18	33	20
10	1	34	27	14	5
23	28	3	12	21	36
2	11	22	35	4	13

Page 32
Snakeword:
Cavernous

Solutions

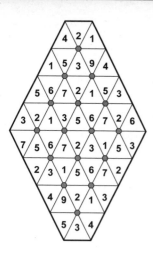

Page 33
Scales:
1 Star and triangle
2 1
3 3

1	0	1	0	0	1	0	1
1	1	0	1	0	1	0	0
0	1	1	0	1	0	1	0
0	0	1	0	1	0	1	1
1	0	0	1	0	1	0	1
1	1	0	0	1	0	1	0
0	0	1	1	0	1	1	0
0	1	0	1	1	0	0	1

Page 34

8	-	6	x	9	18
+	■	x	■	+	
4	x	3	-	7	5
-	■	-	■	x	
5	+	2	÷	1	7
7		16		16	

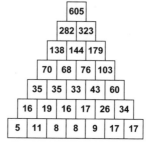

Page 35

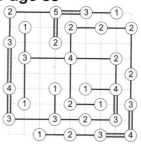

1	5	3	4	6	2
6	4	2	1	5	3
4	2	5	6	3	1
3	6	1	5	2	4
2	1	6	3	4	5
5	3	4	2	1	6

Solutions

Page 36

B3	D1	C5	A4	E2
C1	A2	D4	E3	B5
A5	B4	E1	C2	D3
E4	C3	B2	D5	A1
D2	E5	A3	B1	C4

33	32	30	1	2	3	4
34	35	31	29	10	6	5
36	37	38	28	11	9	7
41	40	39	27	20	12	8
42	49	48	26	21	19	13
43	46	47	25	22	18	14
44	45	24	23	17	16	15

Page 37

| GOOD |
| FOOD |
| FOND |
| FIND |
| HIND |
| HINT |

Snakeword:
Indelible

Page 38

5	4	1	3	2	6
6	2	3	1	5	4
2	6	4	5	3	1
3	1	5	4	6	2
4	5	2	6	1	3
1	3	6	2	4	5

Page 39

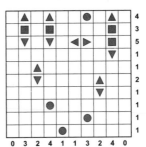

213

Solutions

Page 40

Page 42

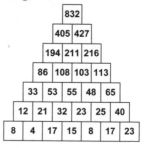

T	E	N	T
E	M	I	R
N	I	C	E
T	R	E	K

Page 41

Hidden Words:
1 Game
2 Serve

Page 43

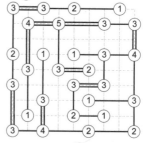

4	1	2	5	6	3
3	5	6	1	2	4
5	4	1	6	3	2
6	3	4	2	1	5
2	6	5	3	4	1
1	2	3	4	5	6

Page 44

Word Scramble:
1. **1** SOMETIMES
2. **2** IMPROMPTU
3. **3** CERTAINLY

3 > 2   5   1   4
∧
4 < 5   1   2 < 3
                ∨
1   3 > 2 < 4   5
        ∧   ∧
2 < 4   3   5   1
        ∧
5   1   4   3 > 2
        ∧   ∧

Page 45

0	0	1	1	0	0	1	1
1	1	0	0	1	0	0	1
1	1	0	1	0	1	0	0
0	0	1	1	0	1	1	0
0	1	0	0	1	0	1	1
1	0	1	1	0	1	0	0
0	1	0	0	1	1	0	1
1	0	1	0	1	0	1	0

B1	E2	C5	A3	D4
C3	A1	E4	D5	B2
E5	D3	A2	B4	C1
D2	C4	B3	E1	A5
A4	B5	D1	C2	E3

Page 46

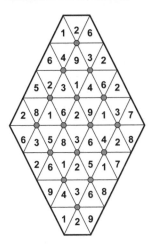

Page 47

3	3	1	6	6	6
3	2	7	7	6	6
6	2	7	7	1	6
6	6	7	7	3	3
6	6	7	6	6	3
6	1	6	6	6	6

Solutions

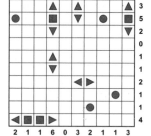

		●	●	●			2
	2	●	4	3	●	●	●
	3			2			2
●	●		2	●	2	1	
	2	2	●		●	2	
			3	●			●
1	●		2	●	2	1	
1	1						

Page 49

		6	4	10	29
	13	2	1	3	7
12	17 30	1	3	4	9
14	2	9	3	9 20	1	8
11	3	8	10 16	3	2	5
30	6	7	9	8		
23	1	6	7	9		

Snakeword:
Expounded

Page 48

B3	E2	D5	A4	C1
E5	D1	C4	B2	A3
C2	A5	B1	D3	E4
D4	C3	A2	E1	B5
A1	B4	E3	C5	D2

Page 50

A	B	U	T
B	O	N	O
U	N	D	O
T	O	O	K

		▲		▲				▲	3
●		■		▼		●		■	5
		▼						▼	2
									0
			▲						1
			▼						1
				◄	►				2
						●			1
					●				1
◄	■	■	►						4

| 2 | 1 | 1 | 6 | 0 | 3 | 2 | 1 | 1 | 3 |

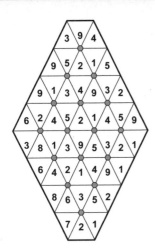

R	A	I	N	E	R	J	O	G
T	S	S	O	R	C	N	I	G
W	A	R	M	U	P	G	S	W
S	G	N	A	S	I	U	M	E
E	Y	M	T	S	N	O	I	A
I	R	P	E	S	M	O	T	T
L	O	P	E	T	H	T	A	I
A	I	B	R	A	G	I	V	N
C	C	O	R	E	I	E	W	G

Page 51

1	6	0	5	3	1	4	1
5	6	0	5	6	2	4	1
5	0	0	4	5	5	3	2
6	6	5	5	0	6	4	3
2	6	4	2	2	1	3	3
1	0	3	1	2	2	4	4
3	3	0	4	2	0	6	1

5 2 > 1 3 4
2 < 3 4 1 5
1 4 > 2 5 > 3
3 1 5 > 4 > 2
4 < 5 3 2 1

Page 53

		8					
6			10				2
						4	
3							
		18					
				6			
				3		3	
	9		2		4		
3						9	
2			8				

2	3	6	5	4	1
5	4	1	3	6	2
3	6	4	1	2	5
1	2	5	6	3	4
4	1	3	2	5	6
6	5	2	4	1	3

Solutions

Page 54

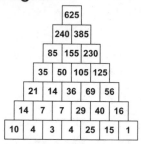

DOGS
LOGS
LAGS
BAGS
BARS
BARK

Page 55

Symbol Values:
Circle = 9
Square = 7
Triangle = 10
Star = 2

Page 56

Word Definer:
2) A fanatic

Wordwheel:
Alligator

Page 57

Word Scramble:
1 BADMINTON
2 DISPENSER
3 REMAINDER

Find the Sum:
32, 33, 43

Page 58

	A	C		C	C	
	A		B		C	
	B	C			A	A
A			A	C	B	
A		A	C	B		B
C	C	B		A		A
				B		

Solutions

1	1	0	1	0	1	0	0
0	0	1	0	1	1	0	1
0	1	1	0	1	0	1	0
1	1	0	1	0	0	1	0
0	0	1	1	0	1	0	1
1	1	0	0	1	1	0	0
1	0	0	1	0	0	1	1
0	0	1	0	1	0	1	1

Page 59

4	3	1	6	2	5
1	5	2	4	6	3
5	2	6	1	3	4
3	4	5	2	1	6
2	6	3	5	4	1
6	1	4	3	5	2

3	2	5	6	1	4
6	3	1	4	2	5
4	5	6	1	3	2
1	4	2	3	5	6
2	1	4	5	6	3
5	6	3	2	4	1

Page 60

5	4	3	2	15	16	17
6	7	1	14	20	19	18
8	9	13	21	22	23	24
10	12	37	36	34	26	25
11	38	48	49	35	33	27
39	42	47	46	45	32	28
40	41	43	44	31	30	29

6	0	0	4	0	1	3	0
4	3	2	1	6	3	5	2
0	2	2	2	5	5	3	6
6	5	4	0	0	5	6	4
1	0	5	3	6	2	1	3
4	1	5	2	6	2	1	3
1	3	4	5	6	1	4	4

Page 61

1	+	3	-	4	0
x		-		-	
8	-	6	-	5	-3
x		x		-	
2	+	7	+	9	18
16		-21		-10	

Symbol Values:
Circle = 1
Square = 5
Triangle = 6
Star = 3

219

Solutions

Page 62

Scales:
- **1** 24
- **2** 6
- **3** 4

Page 63

Wordwheel:
Timetable

Page 64

8	11	20	31	2	13
21	32	9	12	19	30
10	7	36	1	14	3
25	22	33	16	29	18
6	35	24	27	4	15
23	26	5	34	17	28

Word Definer:
1) Shaped like a bunch of grapes

Page 65

C2	B4	E1	A3	D5
A5	E2	C3	D4	B1
E4	D3	B5	C1	A2
B3	A1	D2	E5	C4
D1	C5	A4	B2	E3

0	1	0	1	0	0	1	1
1	1	0	0	1	0	0	1
1	0	1	0	1	1	0	0
0	1	0	1	0	1	1	0
1	0	1	0	1	0	0	1
1	0	0	1	0	1	1	0
0	1	1	0	1	0	1	0
0	0	1	1	0	1	0	1

Page 66

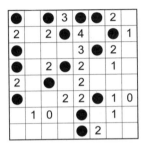

5	4	1	6	2	3
6	2	3	1	4	5
2	1	5	3	6	4
4	3	6	2	5	1
3	6	4	5	1	2
1	5	2	4	3	6

Page 67

LEAF
DEAF
DEAL
DELL
FELL
FALL

Page 68
Find the Sum:
30, 35, 48

Page 69
Hidden Words:
1 Zebra
2 Horse

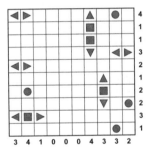

Solutions

6	-	9	x	7	-21
-	■	-	■	+	
5	-	1	-	3	1
+	■	+	■	+	
8	-	2	x	4	24
9		10		14	

3	1	6	2	4	5
1	3	2	6	5	4
4	2	3	5	1	6
6	4	5	3	2	1
2	5	1	4	6	3
5	6	4	1	3	2

Page 71

1	1	0	0	1	0	1	0
0	1	0	1	0	1	0	1
0	0	1	0	1	1	0	1
1	1	0	1	0	0	1	0
1	0	1	0	1	1	0	0
0	0	1	0	1	0	1	1
0	1	0	1	0	0	1	1
1	0	1	1	0	1	0	0

Symbol Values:
Circle = 10
Square = 3
Triangle = 9
Star = 1

Page 72
Snakeword:
Mitigated

			6		
12			9		
					4
	6				
				8	4
2	3		3		
		5			
	20			4	4
			2		
				2	6

Page 73

3	2	4	1	5	6
6	5	1	4	3	2
5	1	6	2	4	3
1	3	2	5	6	4
2	4	3	6	1	5
4	6	5	3	2	1

Wordwheel:
Qualified

Page 74

2	2	5	1	7	7
3	1	5	7	7	7
3	5	5	1	7	7
3	7	5	3	3	6
7	7	7	3	6	6
7	7	7	6	6	6

2 <	3 <	4	5	1
∧ 3	5	∨ 2	1	∧ 4
5 >	4	1	2	∨ 3
∨ 4	1	5	∧ 3	∨ 2
1 <	∧ 2 <	3	∧ 4	5

Page 75
Word Scramble:
   1 TERRITORY
   2 PERMANENT
   3 CONTINENT

23	14	25	2	21	12
26	3	22	13	34	1
15	24	35	30	11	20
4	27	16	33	8	31
17	36	29	6	19	10
28	5	18	9	32	7

Page 76

P	U	M	A
U	P	O	N
M	O	P	E
A	N	E	W

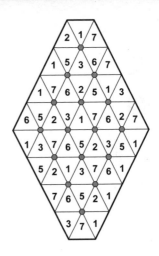

Page 77
Scales:
   1 3
   2 8
   3 12

1	0	0	1	0	1	1	0
0	0	1	1	0	1	0	1
1	1	0	0	1	0	1	0
0	0	1	0	1	0	1	1
1	1	0	1	0	1	0	0
0	1	1	0	0	1	1	0
1	0	0	1	1	0	0	1
0	1	1	0	1	0	0	1

Solutions

Page 78

7	x	5	x	4	**140**
+	■	x	■	-	
6	+	3	x	9	**81**
-	■	-	■	-	
8	+	2	÷	1	**10**
5		**13**		**-6**	

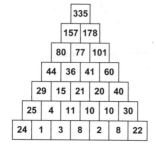

```
                335
             157   178
           80   77   101
         44   36   41   60
       29   15   21   20   40
     25   4   11   10   10   30
   24   1   3   8   2   8   22
```

Page 79

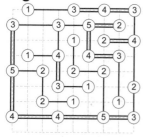

2	1	5	4	3	6
6	4	3	5	2	1
1	6	2	3	4	5
3	5	4	1	6	2
5	3	6	2	1	4
4	2	1	6	5	3

Page 80

C4	E1	A3	B5	D2
D5	C3	B4	E2	A1
A2	D4	E5	C1	B3
E3	B2	D1	A4	C5
B1	A5	C2	D3	E4

11	10	9	8	5	4	3
12	14	15	16	7	6	2
13	18	17	32	33	34	**1**
19	21	31	39	38	37	35
20	22	30	40	47	46	36
23	26	29	41	**49**	48	45
24	25	27	28	42	43	44

Page 81

GONE
LONE
LANE
PANE
PANT
PAST

Snakeword:
Butterfly

224

Page 82

1	6	5	3	2	4
2	4	3	5	6	1
3	1	2	4	5	6
4	2	6	1	3	5
6	5	4	2	1	3
5	3	1	6	4	2

	●		1		2	●
0		3	●			●
	2	●	2	1	2		2
1	●				1	●
		●	1			3	●
	2				●		1
	2	●			2	
	●	2		1	●	2	●

Page 83

	3								4
6			4		6		2	2	
		2						5	
	3				2		2		
					5				
			9		3			2	2
3		5							
3									6
2	2		2			6			
	9								

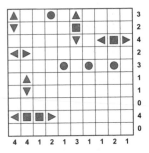

Page 84

1	4	2	5	6	3
3	5	6	2	1	4
6	1	4	3	5	2
2	3	5	6	4	1
4	6	3	1	2	5
5	2	1	4	3	6

Page 85

Hidden Words:
1 Gemini
2 Libra

L	D	H	G	N	I	R	E	T
E	D	U	O	N	Y	O	U	T
R	N	Y	L	C	K	B	Q	A
E	A	C	O	A	R	T	U	H
A	P	M	M	P	I	E	E	C
M	C	O	A	E	B	L	T	H
R	M	T	E	C	R	G	G	C
A	Y	R	T	A	O	G	A	N
W	S	E	T	B	W	D	B	U

Solutions

Page 86

		720			
	358	362			
	185	173	189		
	97	88	85	104	
51	46	42	43	61	
28	23	23	19	24	37
16	12	11	12	7	17	20

S	W	O	T
W	I	R	E
O	R	A	L
T	E	L	L

Page 87

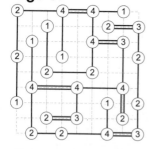

1	3	5	4	6	2
6	1	4	3	2	5
5	2	1	6	3	4
2	4	6	5	1	3
3	5	2	1	4	6
4	6	3	2	5	1

Page 88

Word Scramble:
1 GEOGRAPHY
2 MONITORED
3 EXCEPTION

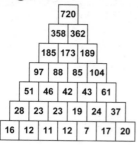

Page 89

1	0	0	1	1	0	0	1
0	1	1	0	1	0	0	1
0	1	0	1	0	1	1	0
1	0	1	1	0	0	1	0
0	1	0	0	1	1	0	1
1	0	1	0	1	0	1	0
0	1	0	1	0	1	0	1
1	0	1	0	0	1	1	0

A5	B3	C4	E2	D1
C3	D2	B1	A4	E5
B2	E4	D5	C1	A3
E1	C5	A2	D3	B4
D4	A1	E3	B5	C2

Solutions

Page 90

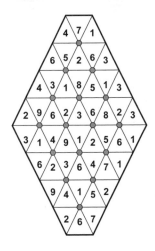

			12	11	
	4 24	3	1		
24 16	7	9	8	17	13
16 7	9	24 7	2	1	4
24 9	8	7 3	16 7	9	
	19 8	2	9		
	10 9	1			

1	●	●		●	●		1
●	2	2		2	2		
2					1		
●		0		2	●		
					3	●	●	1
●	2	●	●		2		2
1			3		1	2	●
	1	●			1	●	2

Page 91

4	4	4	4	7	7
3	3	5	7	7	7
1	3	5	5	7	7
7	7	5	5	1	2
7	7	7	1	4	2
7	7	1	4	4	4

Page 92

A2	D5	B1	E3	C4
C5	A1	D3	B4	E2
D4	B2	E5	C1	A3
E1	C3	A4	D2	B5
B3	E4	C2	A5	D1

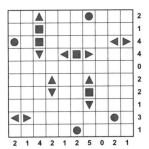

Solutions

Page 93

			5	6	
		3 6	2	1	
	6 16	1	3	2	12 4
10 7	3	12 6	3	2	1
12 9	2	1	16 4	1	3
		19	3	7	9
	17	8	9		

Snakeword:
Sovereign

Page 94

L	A	U	D
A	B	L	E
U	L	N	A
D	E	A	L

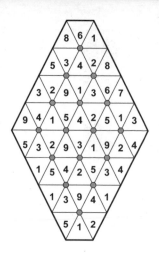

Page 95

4	0	2	2	1	0	5	3
4	3	6	4	5	5	0	6
6	6	2	2	4	4	1	3
4	6	0	4	3	6	5	2
0	2	0	5	1	3	3	1
6	2	6	3	5	3	2	5
4	1	1	0	5	0	1	1

```
1    3 < 4    5    2
                   ^
4    5    2    1    3
v
3 < 4    5    2 > 1
     v         ^
5    2 > 1    3    4
v         ^    ^
2 > 1    3 < 4    5
```

228

Solutions

Page 96

31	6	27	10	29	8
26	17	30	7	20	11
5	32	19	28	9	36
18	25	16	1	12	21
33	4	23	14	35	2
24	15	34	3	22	13

D	K	A	K	N	I	P	A	R
O	R	O	G	N	D	Y	M	T
V	A	N	I	A	A	T	I	I
T	E	G	N	R	B	A	R	N
N	S	E	B	L	R	G	L	I
U	R	K	C	A	A	M	E	M
S	U	S	S	I	A	E	M	O
A	U	Q	I	D	N	L	I	N
L	I	E	T	R	A	C	A	B

Page 97

				4	2	2	2
4				4			
		12	2		3		
			2				
						18	
	2		10				
6	2			12			
	3						
		3		3			4

6	4	3	2	1	5
1	2	5	3	6	4
3	5	1	6	4	2
4	6	2	1	5	3
5	3	6	4	2	1
2	1	4	5	3	6

Page 98

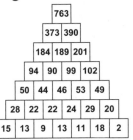

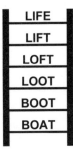

LIFE / LIFT / LOFT / LOOT / BOOT / BOAT

Page 99
Symbol Values:
Circle = 10
Square = 9
Triangle = 2
Star = 1

229

Solutions

Page 100
Word Definer:
2) Entice

Wordwheel:
Excluding

Page 101
Word Scramble:
   1 EAGERNESS
   2 MIGRATION
   3 INCREASED

Find the Sum:
34, 36, 39

Page 102

	B		**C**				
B	B			A	C	C
	A		C	B		
B		B	A	C		**C**
		C	B		A	**A**
C	C	A			B	
		A		**C**	**B**	

1	0	1	1	0	1	0	0
0	1	1	0	0	1	0	1
1	0	0	1	1	0	1	0
0	0	1	1	0	1	1	0
1	1	0	0	1	0	0	1
0	0	1	0	1	0	1	1
1	1	0	1	0	1	0	0
0	1	0	0	1	0	1	1

Page 103

4	5	3	6	1	2
3	2	5	4	6	1
1	3	6	2	5	4
6	1	2	3	4	5
5	6	4	1	2	3
2	4	1	5	3	6

1	4	6	2	5	3
3	5	2	4	1	6
6	2	5	1	3	4
4	3	1	6	2	5
5	1	4	3	6	2
2	6	3	5	4	1

Solutions

Page 104

26	25	24	23	21	1	2
27	29	30	31	22	20	3
28	39	35	34	32	19	4
40	41	38	36	33	18	5
42	43	44	37	17	12	6
47	48	45	16	13	11	7
49	46	15	14	10	9	8

4	6	0	3	5	3	6	1
5	4	5	4	2	2	5	4
1	4	0	2	0	4	6	6
1	1	6	1	2	4	5	2
4	2	3	3	2	1	0	6
0	0	2	0	6	6	5	5
1	3	3	3	3	1	0	5

Page 105

5	+	4	x	6	54
x		+		÷	
9	+	8	+	1	18
x		x		÷	
2	-	7	+	3	-2
90		84		2	

Symbol Values:
Circle = 1
Square = 9
Triangle = 3
Star = 5

Page 106

Scales:
1 2
2 12
3 6

Page 107

Wordwheel:
Professor

Solutions

Page 108

24	31	4	15	18	29
5	16	25	30	3	14
34	23	32	17	28	19
9	6	35	26	13	2
22	33	8	11	20	27
7	10	21	36	1	12

Word Definer:
3) Make a rushing sound

Page 109

E2	A5	B3	D4	C1
B1	C4	D2	A3	E5
A4	B2	C5	E1	D3
D5	E3	A1	C2	B4
C3	D1	E4	B5	A2

1	0	1	0	1	1	0	0
1	0	0	1	0	1	1	0
0	1	0	1	0	0	1	1
0	1	1	0	1	0	0	1
1	0	1	1	0	1	0	0
0	1	0	1	0	1	1	0
0	0	1	0	1	0	1	1
1	1	0	0	1	0	0	1

Page 110

3	4	6	1	5	2
5	2	1	3	4	6
2	1	4	6	3	5
6	5	3	4	2	1
4	6	5	2	1	3
1	3	2	5	6	4

Page 111

NEON
NOON
MOON
MOOD
GOOD
GOLD

Solutions

Page 112
Find the Sum:
11, 12, 20

	1			●	2		
2	●	3		4	●	1	
2	●		●	●		1	
2			2	3		2	
	●			2	●	●	
		2	●	2	3	4	
1	1	1				●	●
●	1		1	●	2		2

Page 113
Hidden Words:
1 Cherry
2 Pear

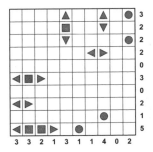

Page 114

8	+	7	x	6	90
-	■	x	■	x	
9	x	2	+	5	23
+	■	+	■	-	
1	-	4	-	3	-6
0		18		27	

1	6	4	2	5	3
6	3	2	5	1	4
5	4	6	3	2	1
2	1	3	4	6	5
4	2	5	1	3	6
3	5	1	6	4	2

Page 115

1	1	0	0	1	0	0	1
1	0	0	1	1	0	1	0
0	0	1	1	0	1	1	0
0	1	1	0	0	1	0	1
1	0	0	1	1	0	0	1
0	1	0	1	0	1	1	0
0	1	1	0	1	0	0	1
1	0	1	0	0	1	1	0

Symbol Values:
Circle = 10
Square = 1
Triangle = 8
Star = 3

233

Solutions

Page 116
Snakeword:
Variation

4		2				4	3		
		2							
4							9		
		8						12	
		8		10					2
					9				
			4						3
	2							3	
	2	4					5		

Page 117

3	1	2	6	5	4
5	2	6	3	4	1
4	5	3	1	6	2
2	4	1	5	3	6
1	6	5	4	2	3
6	3	4	2	1	5

Wordwheel:
Aggravate

Page 118

6	6	7	7	7	7
6	6	6	7	7	7
6	2	1	2	5	5
1	2	3	2	5	5
6	3	3	6	2	5
6	6	6	6	2	1

1 5 2 < 3 < 4

2 < 4 > 3̂ 5 1

3 1 5 4 > 2
^   v
4̂ > 3 1 2̂ 5
v   ^   v   v
5 2 < 4 1 < 3

Page 119
Word Scramble:
1 FIREPLACE
2 HYACINTH
3 MISGUIDED

30	15	20	7	28	13
19	8	29	14	21	6
16	31	18	27	12	35
1	26	9	36	5	22
32	17	24	3	34	11
25	2	33	10	23	4

Page 120

G	R	I	M
R	O	M	E
I	M	P	S
M	E	S	H

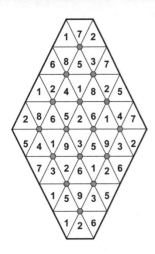

Page 122

5	-	9	-	7	-11
+		-		+	
6	+	8	-	3	11
x		+		x	
1	+	2	x	4	12
11		3		40	

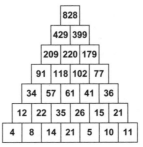

Page 121

Word Definer:
1) A decorative medallion

0	0	1	1	0	0	1	1
1	1	0	1	0	1	0	0
0	1	1	0	1	0	0	1
1	0	0	1	0	1	1	0
1	0	1	0	1	0	0	1
0	1	0	1	1	0	1	0
1	0	1	0	0	1	1	0
0	1	0	0	1	1	0	1

Page 123

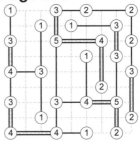

3	1	4	5	6	2
6	2	5	1	3	4
2	5	6	4	1	3
4	3	1	2	5	6
1	4	3	6	2	5
5	6	2	3	4	1

Solutions

Page 124

B1	D3	C2	E5	A4
D2	E1	B4	A3	C5
C3	B5	A1	D4	E2
E4	A2	D5	C1	B3
A5	C4	E3	B2	D1

42	41	39	13	12	10	9
43	44	40	38	14	11	8
45	49	47	37	35	15	7
30	46	48	36	34	16	6
29	31	32	33	18	17	5
27	28	24	23	19	1	4
26	25	22	21	20	3	2

Page 125

ROLL
ROLE
RULE
RILE
RICE
DICE

Snakeword:
Satisfied

Page 126

5	6	4	2	1	3
3	2	1	6	5	4
2	1	6	4	3	5
4	5	3	1	2	6
1	4	5	3	6	2
6	3	2	5	4	1

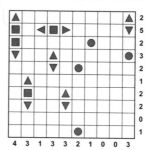

Page 127

Solutions

Page 128

3	1				3	1
9	8	7		8	7	9
	3	1		8	7	9
		3	1	2		
		6	9	2		
	9	3	2		4	8
9	8	7		1	9	3
1	7				2	1

3	4	6	1	2	5
2	5	1	4	3	6
4	6	3	2	5	1
5	1	2	3	6	4
1	3	5	6	4	2
6	2	4	5	1	3

Page 129

Hidden Words:

1 Cousin

2 Uncle

Page 130

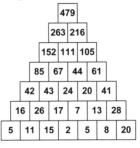

L	A	V	A
A	J	A	R
V	A	N	E
A	R	E	A

Page 131

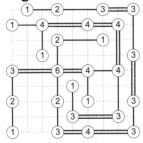

2	6	1	4	5	3
4	5	3	1	2	6
3	1	6	5	4	2
6	3	4	2	1	5
5	4	2	3	6	1
1	2	5	6	3	4

Solutions

Page 132

Word Scramble:

1 NERVOUSLY
2 CURRENTLY
3 BLUEPRINT

3 > 2	1	4 < 5		

3 > 2   1   4 < 5
    ∨   ∨
5   1   2 < 3 < 4
                 ∨
2 < 5   4   1   3
        ∨   ∨
1   4 > 3   5   2

4 > 3   5   2 > 1

Page 133

1	0	0	1	1	0	1	0
0	0	1	0	1	1	0	1
0	1	1	0	0	1	0	1
1	1	0	1	0	0	1	0
1	0	1	0	1	0	1	0
0	0	1	1	0	1	0	1
0	1	0	1	0	1	1	0
1	1	0	0	1	0	0	1

B5	C4	D3	E2	A1
D2	A5	E4	C1	B3
A4	E3	B1	D5	C2
C3	D1	A2	B4	E5
E1	B2	C5	A3	D4

Page 134

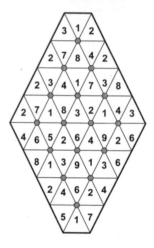

Page 135

13	2	29	22	11	4
30	21	12	3	28	23
1	14	27	34	5	10
20	31	18	9	24	35
15	8	33	26	17	6
32	19	16	7	36	25

Solutions

Find the Sum:
34, 39, 49

Page 136

C	H	E	W
H	I	D	E
E	D	G	E
W	E	E	N

	2		3			3			
2						2			
	2	2				2			
8			6						
				5	2	2			
	2	2				20			
	2						9		
								20	
	4								

Page 137

5	3	1	6	2	4
6	4	2	1	5	3
4	6	5	2	3	1
2	1	3	5	4	6
1	5	4	3	6	2
3	2	6	4	1	5

Wordwheel:
Quotation

Page 138

8	1	6	6	2	2
8	8	6	6	6	1
8	8	8	6	1	6
8	8	5	1	6	6
3	5	5	5	6	6
3	3	5	2	2	6

3   5   2 < 4   1

4 > 2 > 1   5   3

5   1   4   3 > 2

2 < 3   5   1   4

1 < 4 > 3 > 2   5

Page 139

5	x	8	x	4	160
+		+		+	
3	x	1	x	6	18
-		+		-	
2	x	9	x	7	126
6		18		3	

7	10	19	26	1	12
20	27	8	11	18	25
9	6	33	24	13	2
28	21	30	15	36	17
5	32	23	34	3	14
22	29	4	31	16	35

239

Solutions

Page 140

L	I	Z	A
I	V	O	R
Z	O	O	M
A	R	M	Y

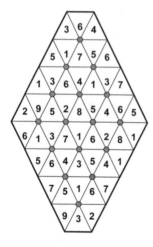

Page 141

Word Definer:
3) A mountain nymph

Page 142

4	-	9	+	5	0
+		x		-	
6	÷	2	-	8	-5
-		÷		x	
7	-	1	-	3	3
3		18		-9	

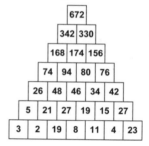

Page 143

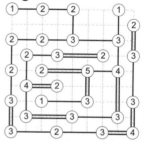

2	1	6	4	3	5
5	4	3	1	6	2
6	3	4	5	2	1
1	2	5	6	4	3
3	6	1	2	5	4
4	5	2	3	1	6

Page 144

B1	A2	E3	C4	D5
C5	B3	D1	E2	A4
D2	E5	B4	A1	C3
E4	C1	A5	D3	B2
A3	D4	C2	B5	E1

4	5	7	8	12	13	14
3	6	9	11	18	17	15
2	1	10	24	23	19	16
40	41	47	46	25	22	20
39	42	48	49	45	26	21
37	38	43	44	32	30	27
36	35	34	33	31	29	28

Page 145

TEEM
DEEM
DEER
DOER
DOUR
POUR

Wordwheel:
Moonlight

Page 146

2	4	1	3	6	5
3	5	6	2	1	4
4	6	2	1	5	3
5	1	3	6	4	2
6	2	5	4	3	1
1	3	4	5	2	6

Page 147

	A		C	
C		A	B	B
B	B	C	A	A
B	A		C	
C	C	B	A	A
A	A		C	B
	A	C	B	

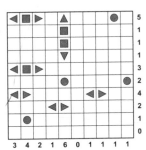

Solutions

Page 148

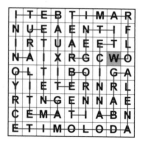

1	5	2	6	4	3
4	6	3	2	5	1
6	2	5	1	3	4
3	1	4	5	2	6
5	4	6	3	1	2
2	3	1	4	6	5

Page 149

Hidden Words:
1 Auburn
2 Scarlet

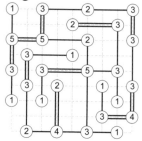

Page 150

Wordwheel:
Zoologist

O	V	I	D
V	I	S	A
I	S	I	S
D	A	S	H

Page 151

4	6	1	2	3	5
3	1	6	5	2	4
1	3	2	4	5	6
6	5	3	1	4	2
2	4	5	6	1	3
5	2	4	3	6	1

Solutions

Page 152

3	2	1	34	33	31	30
4	6	35	36	45	32	29
5	7	37	44	47	46	28
8	18	38	43	49	48	27
9	17	19	39	42	41	26
10	13	16	20	40	25	24
11	12	14	15	21	22	23

3　5　4 > 2 > 1

4^　1　2　5　3

2 < 3　5　1　4^

5　4^　1　3 > 2

1　2^v < 3 < 4^ < 5

Page 153

Find the Sum:
28, 34, 36

A5	B1	E2	C3	D4
D1	E3	C5	A4	B2
C2	D5	B4	E1	A3
B3	C4	A1	D2	E5
E4	A2	D3	B5	C1

Page 154

P	L	A	T
L	U	R	E
A	R	C	S
T	E	S	T

Page 155

25	30	1	16	19	32
2	17	26	31	8	15
29	24	9	18	33	20
10	3	34	27	14	7
23	28	5	12	21	36
4	11	22	35	6	13

Find the Sum:
25, 44, 49

Solutions

Page 156

H	E	M	S
E	V	I	L
M	I	R	O
S	L	O	T

		C	U	T		
	C	U	L	T		
	C	L	O	U	T	
L	O	C	U	S	T	
C	O	N	S	U	L	T
	C	O	U	N	T	S
	S	N	O	U	T	
	S	T	U	N		
		N	U	T		

Page 157

1	3	2	5	6	4
4	5	6	2	3	1
5	2	4	6	1	3
6	1	3	4	5	2
2	6	1	3	4	5
3	4	5	1	2	6

Wordwheel:
Financial

Page 158

1	6	6	6	6	5
7	2	6	6	1	5
7	2	5	1	5	5
7	5	5	5	6	5
7	7	5	6	6	6
7	7	1	6	6	1

4	1	5	3 > 2
3	5 > 2 > 1	4
2 < 3	1	4	5
5	4	3 > 2	1
1	2	4	5	3

Page 159

1	x	4	x	6	**24**
x		-		x	
8	-	5	+	9	**12**
-		x		÷	
2	-	7	x	3	**-15**
6		**-7**		**18**	

29	18	15	4	31	24
14	3	30	25	16	5
19	28	17	32	23	34
2	13	26	35	6	9
27	20	11	8	33	22
12	1	36	21	10	7

Solutions

Page 160

N	A	P	E
A	V	I	D
P	I	N	E
E	D	E	N

Find the Sum:
31, 37, 46

Page 161
Word Definer:
2) Of the cheek

Page 162

6	x	8	x	2	96
x		+		x	
9	-	4	x	5	25
x		+		+	
7	-	3	x	1	4
378		15		11	

0	0	1	1	5	6	0	0
2	3	3	1	2	4	6	2
6	2	1	3	0	4	0	3
5	6	4	2	3	3	2	5
5	1	4	1	3	0	4	0
5	3	2	4	6	5	6	5
4	6	2	1	4	5	6	1

Page 163

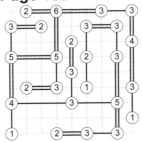

5	2	3	6	4	1
6	4	1	3	2	5
1	6	2	5	3	4
3	5	4	1	6	2
4	1	6	2	5	3
2	3	5	4	1	6

245

Solutions

Page 164

A3	D4	B5	E1	C2
B1	C3	E4	D2	A5
E2	A1	D3	C5	B4
D5	B2	C1	A4	E3
C4	E5	A2	B3	D1

1	3	4	5	6	7	8
2	32	33	34	12	11	9
31	48	47	45	35	13	10
30	49	46	44	41	36	14
26	29	43	42	40	37	15
25	27	28	39	38	19	16
24	23	22	21	20	18	17

Page 165

I	B	I	S
B	I	D	E
I	D	O	L
S	E	L	L

Wordwheel:
Performed

Page 166

5	3	2	4	6	1
2	6	4	1	3	5
4	5	1	3	2	6
1	2	3	6	5	4
3	4	6	5	1	2
6	1	5	2	4	3

2	1	4	5	3	6
3	5	2	6	1	4
6	4	5	3	2	1
1	2	3	4	6	5
5	6	1	2	4	3
4	3	6	1	5	2

Page 167

						A	
C	C		A	B			B
B			B	C	A		A
A	A	C			B		
B		B	C	A			A
B	B	A			C		C
				C			

2	2	4	4	4	1
5	5	5	4	5	5
5	5	1	3	5	5
6	6	3	3	5	4
2	6	6	6	4	4
2	6	2	2	1	4

Solutions

Page 168

4	1	4	4	0	0	3	2
6	0	2	2	4	2	3	6
0	1	5	6	6	3	3	3
0	6	3	1	5	6	1	4
5	1	1	4	2	4	2	3
5	3	4	0	5	2	6	5
1	1	5	0	6	0	2	5

Page 169
Hidden Words:
1 Ghost
2 Goblin

36	35	34	30	29	1	2
37	38	39	33	31	28	3
49	47	45	40	32	27	4
48	46	44	41	26	23	5
17	43	42	25	24	22	6
16	18	19	20	21	10	7
15	14	13	12	11	9	8

Page 170
Wordwheel:
Difficult

P	U	T	T
U	T	A	H
T	A	P	E
T	H	E	N

Page 171

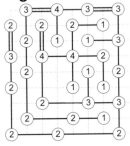

3	5	4	6	2	1
5	3	2	1	4	6
4	2	1	3	6	5
2	1	6	5	3	4
1	6	3	4	5	2
6	4	5	2	1	3

Solutions

Page 172

8	7	4	5	45	46	47
9	10	6	3	44	49	48
11	12	1	2	39	43	42
13	15	16	35	38	40	41
14	17	25	34	36	37	31
18	21	24	26	33	32	30
19	20	22	23	27	28	29

```
[4]  [5]  [3] > [2]  [1]
              ∧
[1]  [2]  [4]  [5]  [3]
      ∧        ∨
[2] < [3]  [1]  [4] < [5]
      ∨        ∨
[5]  [1] < [2] < [3] < [4]
              ∨        ∨
[3] < [4]  [5]  [1]  [2]
```

Page 173

Find the Sum:
28, 35, 39

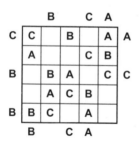

Page 174

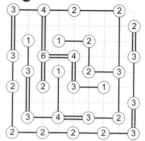

R	I	S	E
I	N	N	S
S	N	A	P
E	S	P	Y

Page 175

2	29	16	13	4	27
17	12	3	28	23	14
30	1	34	15	26	5
11	18	9	24	33	22
8	31	20	35	6	25
19	10	7	32	21	36

Find the Sum:
28, 34, 37

Page 176

B	O	N	E
O	B	O	E
N	O	E	L
E	E	L	S

```
      P  I  T
   T  R  I  P
   T  R  I  P  E
S  P  R  I  T  E
P  E  R  S  I  S  T
P  R  I  E  S  T
   S  P  I  T  E
   T  I  P  S
      S  I  P
```

Page 177

2	3	4	6	5	1
1	6	5	4	3	2
5	1	6	3	2	4
3	4	2	1	6	5
4	5	3	2	1	6
6	2	1	5	4	3

Wordwheel:
Asparagus

Page 178

3	3	2	4	4	4
5	3	2	3	1	4
5	5	1	3	3	7
5	5	6	6	7	7
3	3	6	6	6	7
1	3	6	7	7	7

```
1   3 < 5   4 > 2
                v
4   5   2 < 3   1
v       v
3 > 2   1   5   4
                v
5   1   4 > 2 < 3
        v       ^
2 < 4 > 3   1   5
```

Page 179

1	+	4	x	7	35
+		+		+	
6	+	9	+	3	18
-		x		-	
2	x	5	-	8	2
5		65		2	

12	23	6	29	14	25
7	28	13	24	5	30
22	11	34	15	26	17
35	8	27	18	31	4
10	21	2	33	16	19
1	36	9	20	3	32

Solutions

Page 180

C	A	N	S
A	R	I	A
N	I	B	S
S	A	S	H

Find the Sum:
34, 39, 42

Page 181

Word Definer:
3) An isotope of hydrogen

Page 182

7	x	3	x	2	42
-		-		x	
5	-	4	-	6	-5
x		+		+	
8	+	1	÷	9	1
16		0		21	

2	2	4	0	1	4	4	3
0	6	2	1	0	5	6	3
2	6	4	3	3	5	6	3
1	1	4	6	1	5	0	1
4	4	2	1	3	0	5	2
0	1	6	2	6	5	6	5
0	5	3	4	5	3	2	0

Page 183

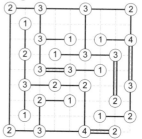

4	4	4	7	7	7
2	4	7	7	7	1
2	1	2	7	3	2
4	4	2	3	3	2
4	4	7	7	7	3
7	7	7	7	3	3

Solutions

Page 184

	C	A	C	B		
C	C			B	A	A
B	B	A	C			
B			B	A	C	
C		C	A		B	B
	A	B		C		
			B			

33	32	31	30	29	27	26
34	35	37	38	39	28	25
11	36	49	46	45	40	24
10	12	47	48	44	41	23
1	9	13	43	42	22	19
2	5	8	14	21	20	18
3	4	6	7	15	16	17

Page 185

L	A	N	D
A	G	U	E
N	U	M	B
D	E	B	T

Wordwheel:
Enhancing

Page 186

6	1	4	2	3	5
2	5	3	6	1	4
1	6	5	4	2	3
4	3	2	5	6	1
3	4	6	1	5	2
5	2	1	3	4	6

5	6	4	2	1	3
6	5	1	3	2	4
2	3	5	1	4	6
3	4	2	6	5	1
1	2	6	4	3	5
4	1	3	5	6	2

Page 187

6	6	6	6	5	1
1	6	6	3	5	5
5	5	1	3	5	5
5	5	4	3	1	2
5	4	4	4	5	2
2	2	5	5	5	5

S A P
G A P S
P A N G S
S P R A N G
R A S P I N G
S P R A Y I N G
S P A R I N G L Y

Solutions

Page 188

		E	R	A		
	C	A	R	E		
R	A	C	E	S		
A	R	C	H	E	S	
R	A	N	C	H	E	S
C	R	A	N	E	S	
S	N	A	R	E		
E	A	R	S			
S	E	A				

0	5	6	1	3	3	4	4
6	2	4	4	2	5	4	4
6	6	2	5	2	0	1	1
2	6	1	0	6	0	5	5
0	6	1	5	0	3	0	1
3	4	5	1	2	2	4	3
3	1	3	5	3	2	0	6

Page 189

Hidden Words:
- **1** Iris
- **2** Pansy

15	16	18	19	30	31	32
14	17	20	29	46	34	33
13	21	28	45	49	47	35
12	22	27	44	48	41	36
11	23	26	43	42	40	37
9	10	24	25	39	38	1
8	7	6	5	4	3	2

Page 190

Wordwheel:
Mistletoe

3	6	6	6	6	7
3	3	6	6	7	7
1	6	7	7	7	7
6	6	6	6	3	6
1	6	1	3	3	6
2	2	6	6	6	6

Page 191

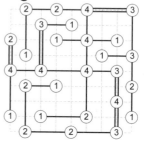

4	2	1	3	5	6
3	6	2	1	4	5
5	1	4	2	6	3
2	5	3	6	1	4
1	4	6	5	3	2
6	3	5	4	2	1

Solutions

Page 192

25	26	28	29	33	34	35
24	27	30	32	38	37	36
18	23	31	39	41	49	48
17	19	22	40	42	46	47
13	16	20	21	43	44	45
12	14	15	8	7	1	3
11	10	9	6	5	4	2

3 > 1   4 < 5   2

1   4   3   2   5

2   5   1   4   3

5 > 3 > 2 > 1   4

4 > 2   5 > 3   1

Page 193

Find the Sum:
10, 11, 26

```
        B  A
C  C        B  A
B     B  A  C        C
B        B  A  C     C
   B  A  C           C
A  A  C        B  B
        C
```

Page 194

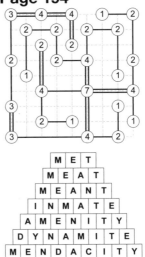

	M	E	T			
	M	E	A	T		
	M	E	A	N	T	
	I	N	M	A	T	E
A	M	E	N	I	T	Y
D	Y	N	A	M	I	T	E
M	E	N	D	A	C	I	T	Y

Page 195

Symbol Values:
Circle = 7
Square = 6
Triangle = 3
Star = 4

Wordwheel:
Reflected

Solutions

Page 196

	A		C	A	
A		A	B	C	
B	B	C	A		
	C			B	A	A
		B		A	C
A	A		C		B
		B	C	A	B

3	6	1	2	5	4
6	2	5	4	1	3
4	1	3	5	6	2
1	5	4	3	2	6
2	3	6	1	4	5
5	4	2	6	3	1

Page 197

2	2	7	7	7	7
4	1	7	7	2	3
4	5	5	7	2	3
4	4	5	5	1	3
2	2	5	1	4	1
3	3	3	4	4	4

```
        S A T
      F A T S
    F A C T S
  C R A F T S
F A C T O R S
F O R E C A S T
F A C T O R I E S
```

Page 198

```
      S U P
    O P U S
  P O U R S
S P R O U T
P O S T U R E
R O U T E S
R O U S E
S O R E
R O E
```

Find the Sum:
15, 22, 28

Page 199
Hidden Words:
1 Hatred
2 Desire

33	34	38	39	40	49	47
32	35	37	41	44	48	46
24	31	36	42	43	45	11
23	25	30	29	28	12	10
19	22	26	27	13	9	8
18	20	21	14	1	7	6
17	16	15	2	3	4	5

Solutions

Page 200

7	7	1	4	4	4
7	7	7	3	4	2
7	1	3	3	1	2
7	9	9	1	6	6
1	9	9	9	6	6
9	9	9	9	6	6

2 5 3 1 < 4
^
3 1 4 2 5
      ^
5 > 4 1 3 > 2
   v   v
4 > 3 > 2 5 1
   v   ^   ^
1 < 2 5 > 4 > 3

Page 201

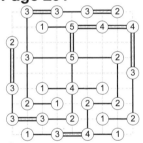

7	22	9	34	5	24
10	33	6	23	16	31
21	8	35	32	25	4
36	11	26	17	30	15
1	20	13	28	3	18
12	27	2	19	14	29

Page 202

	A		C	B	
A		A		C	B	B
B			B	A	C	C
B	B	C			A	
	C		A	B		B
	A	B	C			
	A	B				

```
        N I L
      L I N T
    I N L E T
  T I N S E L
  T I N G L E S
S T E A L I N G
T R I A N G L E S
```

Page 203

Word Definer:
1) A type of sandstone

0	0	1	0	1	1	0	1
1	1	0	0	1	0	0	1
0	0	1	1	0	1	1	0
0	1	1	0	0	1	0	1
1	0	0	1	1	0	1	0
0	0	1	0	1	0	1	1
1	1	0	1	0	1	0	0
1	1	0	1	0	0	1	0

Solutions

Page 204

2	-	6	x	8	-32
+	■	-	■	+	
1	-	9	-	5	-13
x	■	x	■	x	
4	x	7	-	3	25
12		-21		39	

	2	1		●	2		
●	3	●		5	●		0
●	3		●	●	●		
	2	2	2		2	2	●
	●						2
		●	1			●	2
1		1		0	2	●	
●	1					2	●

256